Griffith College

A history of the campus 1...

by John Dorney

with contributions from
Pat McCarthy and Matthew Foyle

GRIFFITH COLLEGE

Published by
Griffith College Dublin, South Circular Road, Dublin 8, Ireland
www.griffith.ie

Copyright © Griffith College Dublin 2013

ISBN 9781906878078

All rights reserved. No part of this publication may be reproduced, stored in a retrieval system, or transmitted, in any form or by any means, electronic, mechanical, photocopying, recording or otherwise, without prior permission in writing of the publisher.

Map on page 8: © Ordnance Survey Ireland/Government of Ireland
Copyright Permit No. MP 0009913

Design & layout by Martin Keaney
www.keaneydesign.ie

Printed by Lettertec Ireland Ltd

Contents

Introduction by Prof. Diarmuid Hegarty — 5

Chapter 1 – The Richmond Bridewell 1813-1892 — 7

Chapter 2 – Wellington Barracks 1892-1922 — 25

Chapter 3 – Griffith Barracks in the Irish Civil War 1922-23 — 39

Chapter 4 – Griffith Barracks 1923-1991 — 55

Chapter 5 – Arthur Griffith — 65

Chapter 6 – From Barracks to College — 71

Bibliography — 90

Introduction

As President of Griffith College it is my honour to welcome you to this book which commemorates the 200th anniversary of the historic buildings on the Griffith College Dublin campus.

As this book outlines, the campus has a varied history. The area was originally known as Grimswood's Nurseries. In 1813 construction began on a remand prison, subsequently known as the Richmond Bridewell, designed to relieve pressure on Newgate Prison. The prison went on to house famous Irish patriots including Daniel O'Connell, James Stephens, Tom Steele and Thomas Francis Meagher.

Prisoners from the 1916 Easter Rising were temporarily held in the jail which was then under control of the War Department. During the Civil War the barracks came under attack a number of times.

Once Ireland had gained independence the site continued to be used as a barracks and was one of the first to be returned to Irish control. The buildings were also used by the Irish Amateur Boxing Association and housed the first unit of the 'Emergency Army'. The Office of Public Works and the Labour Court were both located at this site at different stages until it was sold in 1991 and became Griffith College Dublin.

Since becoming Griffith College Dublin we have sought to combine the rich history of the buildings that surround us with the academic objectives of the College. The site has seen significant investment with student accommodation and a conference centre complementing the original buildings.

In keeping with the history of the site, the campus retains multiple functions with various voluntary bodies utilising the facilities along with other organisations. Now, as Ireland's largest private college with 7,000 students from Ireland and across the world, the campus acts as a centre of the community.

Left: Griffith College – aerial view from 1991.

I would also like to take this opportunity to thank John Dorney and Matthew Foyle for their work in putting this book together and in locating images, and to Pat McCarthy and Brian Maye whose expert advice has supported their endeavours throughout this work.

Finally this year, as we celebrate our 40th Anniversary as an academic institution surrounded by 200 years of heritage, we look forward to developing both as a core of the community and as a centre of education.

Ó bunaíodh an Coláiste rinne muid iarracht go mheabhrú agus a cheiliúradh ár stair agus a fhorbairt i gcónaí le haghaidh ár todhchaí.

Professor Diarmuid Hegarty
President of Griffith College Dublin

Chapter 1
The Richmond Bridewell 1813-1892

Drawing of Daniel O'Connell and the Repeal Martyrs' release and procession from The Richmond Bridewell, 1844.
(Courtesy of the National Library of Ireland)

In the early part of the 19th century the site at what is now Griffith College was used by the Grimwood family as a nursery. For most of the 19th century, however, the site on the South Circular Road was a prison named the Richmond Bridewell. It was designed by the architect Francis Johnston, who also designed the General Post Office, Nelson's Pillar, and part of the Vice-Regal Lodge in the Phoenix Park (now Áras an Uachtaráin) and the interiors of the Custom House. The Richmond Bridewell was built to relieve pressure on the overcrowded Newgate Prison in Dublin.

Construction began in 1811 and continued until 1816, but the new prison was opened in 1813. The initial construction of the buildings cost the city government some £42,000, a very considerable outlay in those times. *Cease to do evil; learn to do well* was the motto over the door of the Richmond Bridewell, leading to the satirical popular nickname for the prison, the 'Cease to Do Evil Hotel'.

Conditions in the early years of the Richmond Bridewell were often brutal. A report of 1827, conducted initially to investigate charges of Protestant proselytizing of Catholic prisoners, revealed a disturbing series of cruel punishments. It found that the following 'cruelties' had been proved; confining prisoners in a piggery day and night, handcuffing, depriving prisoners of blankets, the use of stocks in cold

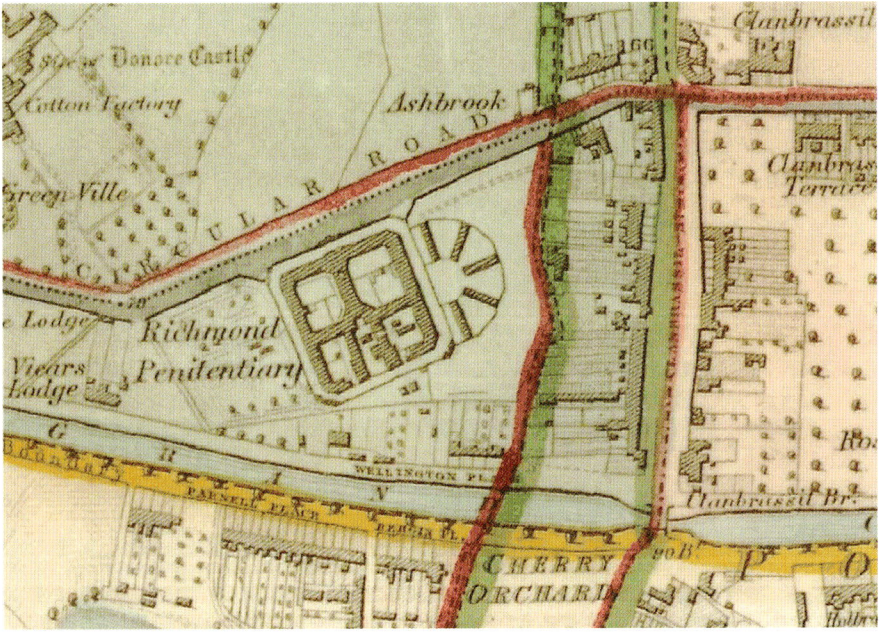

An Ordnance Survey map of 1837 shows the Richmond Bridewell.
(Ordnance Survey Ireland Government of Ireland)

THE RICHMOND BRIDEWELL 1813-1892

A fragment of the original drawings by the architect Francis Johnston, dated 1813. (Courtesy of the Irish Architectural Archive)
Inset: a commemorative coin with the profile of Francis Johnston. (Courtesy of the National Library of Ireland)

weather, confining prisoners in a 'cage' in winter, keeping prisoners on a diet of bread and water as a punishment, gagging, chaining wrists to ankles, use of the 'iron helmet' (a metal device which fitted tightly around the head and face) and 'strait waistcoats' (straitjackets) .

In 1835 a solitary prison building, where prisoners would be confined for bad behaviour, was constructed at the Bridewell at a cost of £8,000. Dublin city borrowed the sum from lenders in Britain and did not pay it back until 1884.

The following year, 1836, another 114 cells were constructed for the main prison at the site at a cost of a further £4,000. Heating by 'hot water ducts' was added in 1837.

The Richmond Bridewell was described in 1837 in the *Topographical Dictionary of Ireland* as:

> *The Richmond Bridewell, on the Circular Road, erected by the city at an expense of £40,000, is a spacious structure enclosed by walls flanked with towers at the angles, and is entered by a massive gateway; between the outer wall and the main building is a wide space, intended for a rope-walk; the interior consists of two spacious quadrangles, the sides of which are all occupied by buildings; the cells, which are on the first floor, open into corridors with entrances at each end; the rooms in the second floor are used as work-rooms; the male and female prisoners occupy distinct portions of the prison; the prisoners not sentenced to the tread-mill are employed in profitable labour, and a portion of their earnings is paid to them on their discharge; they are visited by a Protestant and a R. C. chaplain, a physician, surgeon, and apothecary.*

The accommodation must not have been above criticism, however. In 1838, further work was done, 'rendering the Richmond Bridewell safe for prisoners', while in 1841 there was further building work at the site at a cost of over £6,000.

Above: Daniel O'Connell.

Right: "Richmond Bridewell, late prison of O'Connell and the Repeal Martyrs", from The Freeman's Journal.

(Courtesy of the National Library of Ireland)

Daniel O'Connell's stay in the Richmond Bridewell

A very far cry from the lot of the ordinary inmate in the prison was the experience there of the nationalist leader Daniel O'Connell, who was held in the Bridewell for three months in 1844. He was arrested after his proposed 'Monster Meeting' at Clontarf in favour of the repeal of the Act of Union or Irish self-government was declared illegal. On the night of Saturday, October 7, 1843, a proclamation was issued from Dublin Castle banning the meeting, written by the Prime Minister of Britain and Ireland, Sir Robert Peel. It called the proposed meeting for the restoration of the Irish Parliament, abolished in 1801, "an attempt to overthrow the constitution of the British Empire as by law established".

O'Connell was charged with, 'conspiracy to raise and create discontent and disaffection among the Queen's subjects', and a number of other counts to the effect that he had desired to dissolve the

Union between Britain and Ireland and to establish an alternative judiciary in Ireland. He was tried in early 1844 before a jury that he alleged was 'packed' with Protestants and unionists. O'Connell maintained he had merely pursued legitimate political goals by open and legal means but was nevertheless found guilty of conspiracy and in March of that year he was sentenced to twelve months imprisonment. An angry mob of O'Connellite supporters barracked the carriage that took their leader from the Four Courts to the Richmond Bridewell.

O'Connell's stay there was, however, much more comfortable than that of most ordinary prisoners. He and his supporters who had been imprisoned (including his son John and right-hand-man 'Honest' Tom Steele) were housed in rooms in the Governor's suite, which was described as, 'a pleasant country house, situated in the middle of extensive grounds, bright with fair women and the gambols of children, with abundant means either for study or amusement'.

The reason for their comfortable accommodation was that the prison was under the control of Dublin Corporation, a body dominated by O'Connell's supporters, who just three years earlier had elected him Lord Mayor of the city. They instructed that special care and attention be given to, 'our illustrious countryman'. O'Connell was free to

Daniel O'Connell addressing crowds from the balcony of his home in Merrion Square following his release from The Richmond Bridewell, 6 September 1844. (Courtesy of the National Library of Ireland)

Above: view of Richmond Bridewell and, below, the Dining Room, as drawn by Henry O'Neill R.H.A. 1844.
(Courtesy of the Christian Brothers, Edmund Rice House)

Above: the Liberator's bedroom and, below, John O'Connell's bedroom, Richmond Bridewell, as drawn by Henry O'Neill R.H.A. 1844. Both rooms display an opulence not usually accorded an inmate of the prison.
(Courtesy of the Christian Brothers, Edmund Rice House)

Section of the Register from the Richmond Bridewell 1845-1849.

No.	NAMES.	County.	Crime.	Sentence of Transportation for	Convicted. Where, and before whom tried.	Convicted. When.	Age.	Height Feet.
70	Thomas Deane	Kings Co	Highway Robbery	7 years		5th March 1847	24	
71	John Thomas	Do	Larceny	7 years		25th October	20	
72	William Harrison	Do	Larceny	7 years		25th October	26	
73	John Nugent	Do	Assault &c. & Fueling	7 years	Justice Doherty	25th July 1848	30	5
74	James Corcoran	Do	Demolishing a House	7 years		25th July 1848	24	
75	Thomas Egan	Do	Maiming Cattle	7 years	Judge Doherty	28th July 1848	20	5
76	George Troy	Do	Perjury	7 years	Assistant Barrister	29th March	35	5
77	John Egan	Do	Assault & Robbery	7 years	Same	3rd April	26	
78	William Allaway	Do	Assault so as to Endanger Life	7 years	Same	1st January 1849	25	
79	Thomas Moran	Kildare Co	Burglary & Robbery	7 years		3rd August 1847	21	
80	John Byrne	Do	Larceny	7 years		31st Dec.	25	
81	Myles Woods	Leitrim	Lamb Stealing	7 years	Assistant Barrister	30th March 1848	19	
82	Dominick Brennan	Do	Stealing a Skillet	7 years		5th April	42	
83	Patrick McKiernan	Do	Appearing armed by Night	7 years		1st March 1847	26	

GOVERNMENT PRISON.

Colour of			Married or Single.	Read or Write.	Trade.	Religion	When Committed.	Disposed of.		OBSERVATIONS, Character, &c.
Eyes.	Hair.	Complexion.						When.	How.	
			Married		Labourer		3rd March 1849	20th April 1849	Spike Island	Good.
			Single		Cooper	"	"	" 7th May	Em'd Ship Hyderabad	Good
			Single		Shoemaker (Stonecutter)	"	"	" 7th May	Em'd Ship Hyderabad	Good
Brown	Brown	Fresh	Married 1 child	Neither	Labourer	"	"	" 30th July	Em'd Ship Havering	Bad. Good in Gaol not convicted before
			Single		B. Smith	"	"	" 31st March 1849	Spike Island	Bad. Good in Gaol not convicted before
Brown	Brown	Fresh	Single	Neither	Labourer	"	"	" 30th July	Em'd Ship Havering	Bad. Good in Gaol not convicted before
Blue	Brown	Fresh	Married 4 children	Reads	Labourer	"	"	" 30th March 1849	Spike Island	Bad. Good in Gaol not convicted before
Blue	Brown	Fresh	Married 4 children	Neither	Labourer	"	"	" 30th July	Em'd Ship Havering	Bad. Good in Gaol not convicted before
Grey	Brown	Fresh	Single	R & W	Shoemaker	"	"	" 15th February 1850	To Trustees	Good. Best character Industrious
			Single		Labourer	"	"	" 30th March 1849	Spike Island	Bad
			Single		Labourer	"	"	" 15th March "	Smithfield Sick	Bad one
Brown	Red	Fair	Single	Neither	Labourer	"	"	" 20th May 1850	Discharged	Good Industrious
			Married		Labourer	"	"	" 18th May 1849	Em'd Ship Hyderabad	Good Industrious
			Single		Labourer	"	"	" 7th May	Em'd Ship Hyderabad	Good Industrious
			Married		Labourer	"	"	" 7th May	Em'd Ship Hyderabad	Very Good

THE RICHMOND BRIDEWELL 1813-1892

receive guests and his dinner table was never set for less than 30 people. He even became infatuated with one visitor, the 23 year old Rose McDowell (daughter of a political ally), whom the 68 year old O'Connell asked to marry him (she refused).

In September 1844, O'Connell's conviction was struck down in the House of Lords due to the jury having been improperly selected. He was freed on September 5, 1844, whereupon hundreds of his jubilant supporters descended on the Richmond Bridewell in celebration. O'Connell, ever the master of political street theatre, returned to the prison from his home in Merrion Square that evening for a formal procession home, where his release could be openly celebrated by thousands of Repealers.

The Famine

Not long after O'Connell's dramatic release from the Richmond Bridewell, Ireland was afflicted by perhaps the greatest human catastrophe in its history, the Great Famine which killed some one million people between 1845 and 1848, mostly in the rural west and south of the country.

In Dublin, where the poor generally lived on bread rather than potatoes, the results of the Famine were more indirect. While the population of Ireland fell by as much as 1.5 million in the Famine years, the population of Dublin actually increased from 232,726 in 1841 to 258,361 in 1851, as refugees from the hungry provinces descended on the capital.

Famine in Ireland 1845-48. The Richmond Bridewell was filled to twice its capacity during the Famine. (Courtesy of the National Library of Ireland)

Workhouses and prisons such as the Richmond Bridewell became crammed with desperate, starving people – in the former seeking the only form of state aid available and in the latter for petty crimes such as theft. Indeed, there were several organised attacks on bread shops by 'country people' fleeing the Famine. Whereas in 1845 there were only 627 people in custody in all of Ireland, in 1853 there were over 4,000.

It was recorded that the Liberties district, just north of the Richmond Bridewell, was 'crowded with fever stricken strangers from different parts of the country, especially Mayo, Galway and other western counties'. Mainly as a result of the spread of contagious diseases caused by the Famine refugees, burials rose by some 20% in Dublin during the Famine and there were an estimated 20,000 excess deaths in the Irish capital between 1841 and 1851. The prison records show a total of 154 deaths occurring in the prison from 1845 – 1849.

The Richmond Bridewell in 1858 was reported to have housed 60 men and 41 women. They were generally low risk prisoners, described in the language of the time as, 'debtors, criminals, drunkards and lunatics'.

The type of inmate typically imprisoned in the Richmond Bridewell is illustrated by a court report from *The Irish Times* of May 5, 1859. A young man, named James Daly, who had two previous convictions for larceny, was convicted of stealing a brass bar from a tea shop in South Great George's Street. His father, described in the press report as 'a respectable hard working tradesman', pleaded for 'merciful treatment'. The unimpressed judge, however, sentenced James Daly to three months imprisonment in the Richmond Bridewell and recommended he be sent to a reformatory when he got out.

Discipline inside the Richmond Bridewell was strict. In 1859 it was noted that eleven prisoners were sentenced to solitary confinement and two to whipping. The other prisoners had to do work such as picking oakum (a form of tarred fibre used in shipbuilding) or, for special punishment, walking on treadmills.

The Fenian Era

O'Connell was not the last Irish nationalist leader to be held in the Richmond Bridewell. Other prominent nationalists imprisoned there included leaders such as William Smith O'Brien and Thomas Francis Meagher, who were held there for their part in the abortive 1848 Young Ireland rebellion, a poorly planned episode that occurred at the tail end of the Great Famine. Meagher unveiled the Irish tricolour of green white and orange in March 1848 in his native Waterford – a gift from French republicans. The flag was later adopted as the symbol of the Irish Republic after 1916. Both men were sentenced to death and imprisoned in the Richmond Bridewell in 1849 (like O'Connell they were held in the Governor's Residence), but were reprieved due to a public outcry and sentenced instead to transportation to Australia. Meagher later made his way to America where he led an Irish brigade in the American Civil War. After the Civil War had ended, Meagher became acting Governor of Montana.

The most famous Irish nationalist activist imprisoned in the Richmond Bridewell in the post Famine era, however, was the Fenian leader James Stephens. Stephens, who had been wounded in the ill-fated insurrection of 1848, founded the Irish Republican Brotherhood (IRB) or Fenian Brotherhood in 1858, which was dedicated to the pursuit by any means necessary of an independent Irish republic. In 1865, government officials raided the IRB headquarters in Dublin, housed in the office of the Fenian newspaper the *Irish People*. Most of the leaders were arrested, convicted of treason and felony, and

James Stephens, Fenian leader.
(Courtesy of the National Library of Ireland)

sentenced to penal servitude. Stephens avoided immediate arrest but was picked up and charged with conspiracy and high treason and was imprisoned in the Richmond Bridewell.

However, on November 5th, 1865, a distressed Daniel Ryan, Superintendent of the Dublin Metropolitan Police, wrote to his superiors: "I beg to state that at 5.20 o'clock this morning a constable of E. Division stated at G. Division office that Mr. Marquess, Governor of the Richmond Bridewell, directed him to call and say that James Stephens, who was confined there on a charge of high treason, had made his escape".

Security in the Richmond Bridewell seems to have been rather lax. Stephens had been able to open his cell and then, by stacking two tables one on top of the other, to have simply climbed over the boundary wall. To do this he had to open seven locked doors, which he had done by means of what the police described as 'false keys'. It seemed certain to the investigating authorities, therefore, that Stephens had some help from prison staff in his escape and indeed he did. Daniel Byrne and John Breslin, who were members of the prison staff and also Fenians, had a replica key made for Stephens and stacked the tables near the prison wall so that he could make good his escape.

Stephens subsequently fled to France and then to America. His escape made world headlines in 1865, including the front page of *Harper's Weekly* in America. *The New York Times*, for its part, reported:

> *Our Dublin correspondent, in his letter of last night, says: "The Richmond Bridewell, from which the Fenian chief, JAMES STEPHENS, has escaped ... is situated upon the Circular road, an avenue that almost surrounds the City of Dublin.... It is not the best protected of the Dublin prisons, and it is remarked that if STEPHENS had been placed in Kilmainham he could not have got off...*
>
> *A reward for the apprehension of STEPHENS of £1,000 will, I understand, be offered by the Executive to-night, and also one of £300 for the apprehension of the person or persons who aided his escape, or such information as will fasten the guilt upon them. All sorts of rumors of an absurd character are of course afloat; one has got many to credit it, that a strange steamer has been lying off shore in the bay, awaiting STEPHENS, which, it need hardly be said, is quite impossible. According to another rumor, STEPHENS was met and carried off when he crossed the prison wall, by a hundred or more armed Fenian Brothers.*

Stephens' escape became a well-known story among Dubliners thereafter. Joseph O'Connor, an IRA prisoner in what was then Griffith Barracks in 1922, recalled:

Harper's Weekly front cover, 7th April 1866.

Caption reads: 'Richmond Bridewell, Dublin, from which head-centre Stephens escaped.'

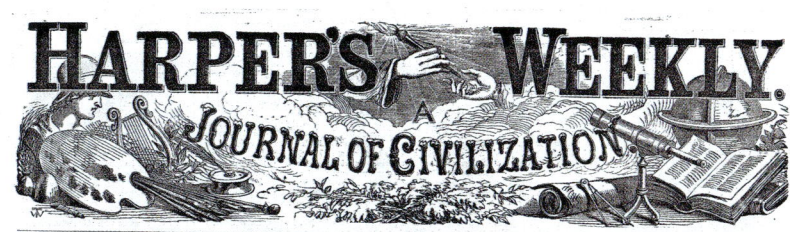

> *While a prisoner in Griffith I got my last sight of my father. He was looking through the main gate, hoping to catch a glimpse of me. We saw each other then for the last time on earth. When I was a boy he had pointed out to me the cell in the same building he occupied during Fenian times, and then he would show me where he was posted when James Stephens, the Fenian Leader, escaped from the same prison.*

Stephens was not, however, the only Fenian to be held in the Richmond Bridewell. After the failed uprising which the organisation attempted in 1867, several were imprisoned at the Richmond Bridewell. They found conditions there, which were made stricter after Stephens' embarrassing escape, harsh, and certainly a far cry from those experienced by Daniel O'Connell. According to one account, "Lumped together with other inmates, the Fenian prisoners found that they were obliged to sleep on hard plank beds rather than hammocks and they were introduced to mindless, repetitive tasks such as oakum picking and walking on treadmills". Another distinguished inmate in the Richmond Bridewell was the Lord Mayor of Dublin, Timothy Daniel Sullivan, who was imprisoned there for two months for publishing *The Nation*, an Irish nationalist newspaper, in 1887.

The Richmond Bridewell in 1870

In 1877, when the British Government established a General Prisons Board in Ireland to centralise the organisation of all gaols and prisons, the convict population in all of Ireland was 4,000 men and women, divided amongst 38 county prisons, 96 bridewells like Richmond, and four convict prisons.

What was daily life like in the Richmond Bridewell? A look at an inspector's report of 1870 gives us some insights.

A statutory inspection on December 19, 1870 found that Richmond housed 245 adult male prisoners (by this time female prisoners were not housed in Richmond, being all accommodated in Grangegorman) along with twelve juveniles. The total was an increase on the previous year, but remained within the norm for Richmond's convict population in the 1860s, which hovered between 200 and 250 throughout the decade. Of those in Richmond in late 1870, 23 were awaiting trial and eleven were military prisoners, having been tried by courts martial. Of the remainder, 48 were there for some form of larceny or theft, 44 for 'other misdemeanours', eight in default of bail, seventeen for non-payment of fines, one under the Poor Law Act and five were 'drunkards'.

A handful of inmates had committed serious crimes such as manslaughter or illegal stockpiling of weapons (presumably Fenian activists) but the great majority were there for either theft, common assault or drunkenness. Many of these were serving short sentences. In 1870, a total of 3,296 prisoners were committed to Richmond, but only 245 were there on the day of inspection, meaning that most served only a short period inside the gaol. In 1870 the highest number in Richmond on any given day was 341 on July 26. Only 45 prisoners out of 245 present on the day of inspection were serving sentences of a year or over.

Most prisoners were housed in cells with two other inmates. The heating system was described as 'imperfect' but there was, apparently 'ample water', and inmates could have a bath twice a month. Generally, however, they washed in sheds in the yard. Gas heated the cells until 7:30 pm in winter time. They were paraded for breakfast at 8.00 am and locked back in their cells at 6.00 pm. In between they performed hard labour and other tasks involved in the running of the prison such as cooking and cleaning.

The inspectors reported that security had improved since Stephens's escape five years earlier and that 'discipline is very efficiently maintained'. Photographs were taken of some inmates, especially repeat offenders, 'professional thieves and the criminal class'.

Infractions on the part of prisoners were still punished by time on the treadmill, solitary confinement and punitive labour. Prisoners' food was also stopped on occasion, but whipping, noted in the 1860 report, appears to have stopped by this date. Some 29 prisoners attended school regularly.

After 1868, the Richmond Bridewell became a site of execution. In 1868, the law was changed so that executions were no longer performed in public. The first private execution in Dublin, after the passing of the 1868 Act, was of one Andrew Carr on July 28, 1870 in the Richmond Bridewell. He was an army pensioner who voluntarily confessed to cutting the throat of his girlfriend during a drunken argument. Present at his execution were thirteen newspaper reporters, three Catholic priests and three 'medical gentlemen'. The governor was uneasy about the hangman (like Carr an ex-soldier) who was inexperienced at his grim new job. He decided on a drop of fourteen feet for the prisoner despite advice from the surgeon that eight feet would suffice. At the drop, Andrew Carr's head was ripped from his body. According to *The Irish Times*, "the head sprang off from the body against the wall, blood spouted and spattered all around and the trunk fell into a pool of it on the ground. The body quivered slightly for about three minutes after the execution".

A December 1870 report concluded: "the lamentable occurrence at the execution of Carr was caused by the want in elasticity of the rope".

The execution of Joseph Poole

Executions were relatively rare in late 19th century Dublin, but the Richmond Bridewell did witness one more, very high profile hanging. In late 1883, it was the scene of the execution of Joseph Poole, a member of the Irish Republican Brotherhood. He was executed at a time when Fenian political violence was causing both outrage and fear among the political establishment in Ireland. The Invincibles, a militant Fenian grouping, assassinated the two leading members of the British administration in Ireland, the Chief Secretary for Ireland, Frederick Cavendish and the Under Secretary for Ireland, Thomas Henry Burke, in the Phoenix Park on May 6, 1882. Five Invincibles were later hanged for this crime.

Joseph Poole.
(Courtesy of Robert Delaney)

Poole was, a rank and file member of the Fenians in Dublin. He was sworn into the IRB in 1873, aged just 18 and worked for most of his life as a tailor. By 1882 he was also armourer (or quartermaster) for a Fenian circle or cell. He was arrested in July 1882 and charged with the killing of John Kenny, a Fenian and an alleged police informer, who was suspected of giving away the Invincibles. It was alleged that Poole was a member of a Fenian group known as the 'Vigilance Committee', which was tasked with eliminating informers, though he denied this. Poole admitted drinking with Kenny on the night of his death but denied any part in his murder. However, a witness at Poole's trial (a roommate of his) later alleged that Poole returned to his lodgings that night saying, 'Kenny will tell no more'. He was released for lack of evidence.

Poole was rearrested in December 1882 and charged again with Kenny's murder. It was believed that the Dublin Metropolitan Police (DMP) sought the death penalty as they suspected that Poole had a hand in shooting dead one of their constables earlier that year. The shooting of this policeman had occurred as a result of a clash between two rival Fenian factions in 1882 – one backers of the IRB's Supreme Council, the other, Poole's faction, Stephenites (followers of the exiled leader James Stephens). The Council faction were trying to kill Poole in a dispute over who controlled weapons caches in Dublin. Shots were exchanged in the streets after a dispute over which faction would control a cache of weapons. The only casualty, however, was a DMP policeman named Cox, who was shot inadvertently when he tried to intervene. A Fenian named Dowling was later charged with the shooting and served ten years in prison.

When Poole stood trial for the killing of John Kenny, the Crown produced as a witness Poole's own brother-in-law, William Lamie, a former Fenian, who testified to the factional divisions within the Dublin Fenian movement and on Poole's role in the 'Vigilance Committee'. However, the case collapsed with the jury being unable to reach a verdict. A second trial was quickly arranged and the jury was 'packed' with government supporters in order to ensure a conviction and despite no new evidence being presented, he was duly sentenced to death on November 20th, 1883. His father was reported to have wept at the verdict and shouted "Joe, Joe", to which Poole replied, "Keep up father, keep up, I am ready to die".

Upon hearing his sentence of death, Poole told the court: "I believe it is on account of being an enemy, humble as I am, of the Government under which I have the misfortune to live, that I have been persecuted in the manner I have been. Still I am not afraid to die, or ashamed of what has brought me to the scaffold. It is not for murder, it is for being a member of the Irish Republican Brotherhood that has brought me to the scaffold, and I am prepared to die for it". He called from the dock for "Three Cheers for the Irish Republic and to Hell with English tyranny!"

Poole was hanged in the Richmond Bridewell on December 18th, 1883. The executioner was a man named William Jones from Wales. Poole was attended by a priest named Father Donnegan and was reported to have shown "the utmost fortitude" on the scaffold, "never for a moment ceasing to utter the response to the prayers" of the priest. He died instantly on being hung, the drop from the scaffold breaking his neck. When Poole was hung a black flag was raised over the walls of the prison. The watching crowd, according to the press, gave 'a wailing cry'. Poole's body was buried in an unmarked quicklime grave within the prison.

Poole's case became a notorious example of injustice in Ireland in the 1880s, as it was widely believed that he was innocent of the crime for which he was convicted and that the verdict had been achieved by 'packing' the jury. The Irish Parliamentary Party, at that time agitating for Home Rule, brought up Poole's innocence in the House of Commons. However, public opinion was really roused on the matter when allegations that Poole's conviction had been secured by perjury came to light. Frank Grundy, a Fenian and a friend of Poole, on completion of a two year prison sentence in August 1884, made a deposition claiming that he had been twice approached by the authorities whilst incarcerated, and offered freedom if he falsely implicated Poole in the killing of John Kenny. Grundy said that he had refused. Nor was this the only allegation of attempts by Dublin Castle to use perjury to secure Poole's conviction. In his speech from the dock, Joseph Poole himself had mentioned Lizzy Kearns, Grundy's sweetheart, who had been approached by DMP Superintendent John Mallon and offered her boyfriend's freedom if she swore falsely, but she too had refused.

A plaque erected to Poole's memory in Griffith Barracks in 1968.

Poole, the second and the last man to be hanged in the Richmond Bridewell, therefore became a potent symbol of misgovernment in 19th century Ireland.

During work on the site in the 1890s, as part of its conversion into Wellington Barracks, Joseph Poole's body was discovered in a casket marked 'J.P.'. His father had died shortly beforehand, but Poole's step-mother and sisters petitioned Dublin Castle to be allowed to reclaim the body and give it a proper burial. On the advice of John Mallon of the DMP, their request was turned down. Poole's body was instead reburied in another anonymous site within the Barracks.

The Poole family maintained their republican tradition. Four of his brothers served in the Irish Citizen Army during the Easter Rising of 1916. In 1958, three of Poole's younger brothers, by that time quite elderly, approached the Irish Army garrison at what was by then Griffith Barracks in order to try to exhume Poole's remains and give him, belatedly, a decent burial. The soldiers in Griffith could not give them permission to do so, but they returned some weeks later with an exhumation order from the Department of Defence. However, despite a day of digging behind the barracks' gymnasium, they sadly found only an animal bone.

A plaque was erected to his memory in Griffith Barracks in 1968 by the National Graves Association. In 2007, following correspondence between the Poole family and Diarmuid Hegarty, President of Griffith College, the plaque, which had been kept in storage, was re-erected.

From prison to barracks

In 1877, the Richmond Bridewell was commandeered by the War Office under the Military Prisons Act of that year, as a site for a future barracks, but it was not occupied by troops until the 1890s. The initial cost of the conversion work was £40,000 and another £25,000 was ploughed into erecting an officers' mess and living quarters.

The City of Dublin, in 1892, sued the War Department for compensation, claiming that the tax-payers of the city had put over £96,000 into the Bridewell since its foundation in 1813. The War Office replied that under the 1877 General Prisons Act, as the site had been used as a prison while War Office property up to 1887, the Corporation was not entitled to any compensation.

The Corporation had a minor success, however, in claiming that portions of the site belonged to them and the War Office eventually agreed to pay them an annual rent of £28. Additionally, £137 had to be paid to the Treasury and £300 to the Grand Canal Company for access to the canal at the rear of the complex. Further rents had to be paid to two private citizens, I.S. Winter and Jack Doyle, who owned portions of the site and were respectively paid £83 and £14 per annum.

In 1892, after extensive re-building work, the Richmond Bridewell, now renamed Wellington Barracks after the Duke of Wellington, was occupied by troops of the Royal Munster Fusiliers, though re-building was not completed until 11 November 1893. It would be garrisoned by British troops up to 1922.

Chapter 2
Wellington Barracks 1892-1922

Wellington Barracks with soldier on guard duty, c.1900.
(Courtesy of the National Library of Ireland)

On December 12, 1891, at 8 o'clock in the morning the 1st Battalion, Royal Munster Fusiliers under the command of Colonel Johnston disembarked at Kingstown (now Dun Laoghaire) from *HMS Assistance* and marched to their new quarters at Wellington Barracks, on the site of the old Richmond Bridewell. They were the first troops to be housed there, beginning almost a century of military use.

When the Munsters marched in, building work was still underway, so the soldiers had to share the site with construction workers, who did not finish their work until 11 November 1893.

The Munsters were relieved in late 1892 by the 2nd Battalion of the Duke of Cornwall's Light Infantry. After the Cornwall Light Infantry, Wellington was occupied by battalions from the Sussex Regiment, and the North Staffords before the Munsters and Cornwalls were rotated through again. From 1900 it was garrisoned by the King's Liverpool Regiment, The East Lancashire Regiment, a battalion of the Dublin Fusiliers in 1910, the Royal Fusiliers in 1912, the East Surrey Regiment in 1914 and the Royal Irish Fusiliers in 1917.

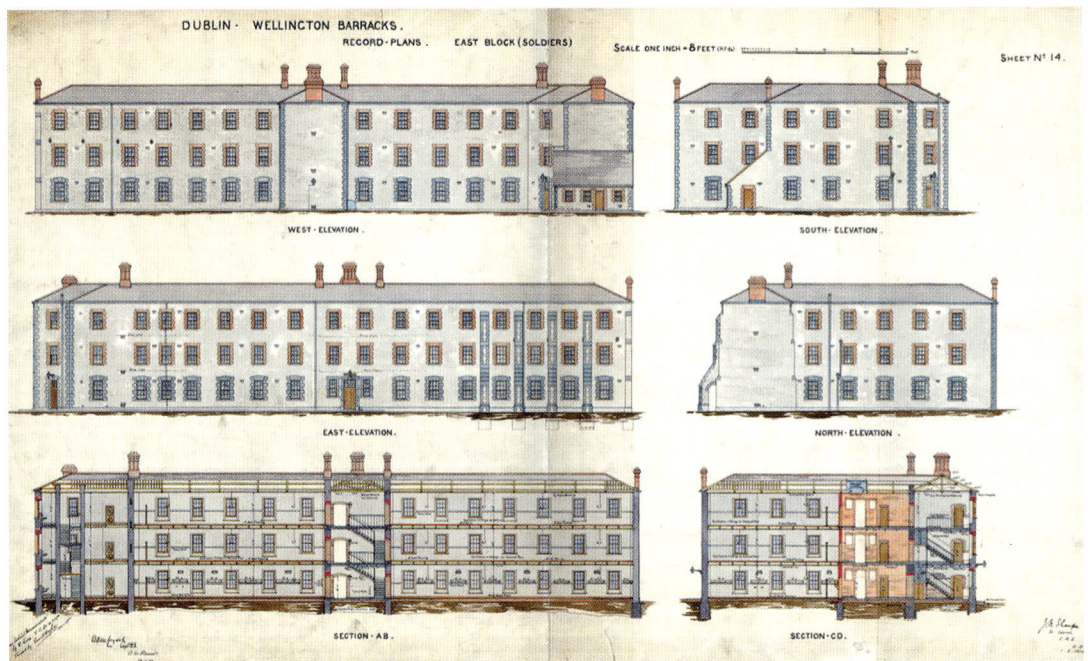

Wellington Barracks, plan/elevations c. 1900. (Courtesy of Military Archives, Department of Defence)

Inside Wellington Barracks, with soldiers on horseback c.1900. (Courtesy of the National Library of Ireland)

Wellington was designed for occupation by a battalion of about 600 men. Most troops lived in single soldiers' quarters, based in the old cell blocks. However a considerable number lived with their families in the married quarters. The 1911 census returns show 41 families, or around 200 people, living in the married quarters. One such family, for instance, were the McMurrays. The head of the household was Robert, a 38 year old soldier who had been born in Belfast. His English-born wife Elizabeth, ten years his junior, had borne him six children, of whom all but the youngest two, aged 2 and 4 respectively, could read and write. All had been born in England and belonged to the Church of England.

Daily life in the barracks was a routine of guard duty, inspections and parades, punctuated by war simulations or manoeuvres and sport. In 1893 for example, it was reported:

> 'An Invading force under the command of Major Fisher, 10th Hussars, Marlborough Barracks (drill order with full dress headdress) was landed near Wicklow on 16th December. It will march north on Dublin under Lt. Col. Courtney, 1st Royal Sussex Regiment, Wellington Barracks (drill order) will take up a line of outposts on the probable line of the invaders' advance the outposts to be in position by 9:15 a.m.'

Two years later, units from Wellington also took part in the Royal Irish Military Tournament in Ballsbridge, which included displays such as Trooping the Colour, Musical Rides and a March Past, as well as competitions such as, tent pegging, lemon cutting, wrestling on horseback, boxing and tug of war, among others. Troops were also kept busy with more conventional team sports. In 1899, the soccer team of the North Staffords, quartered in Wellington, defeated the Scottish Borderers 4-1 in the Irish Army Cup. Officers, however, were free to pursue more genteel activities. Two captains, Dease and Prouse, were reported to have acted in a 'screaming farce' entitled A night on the Sugar Loaf, at the Rotunda Military Fete.

British Army Parade in Dublin. (Courtesy of the National Library of Ireland)

Troops from the barracks were also involved in ceremonial duties such as displays for the coronation of British monarchs and parading for Royal visits to Dublin; by Edward VII in 1903 and 1904, and by George V in 1911.

The Great War

However, the relatively sedate life of the troops garrisoned at Wellington was shattered by the outbreak of the First World War in August 1914. The day after Britain's declaration of war, on August 5 1914, *The Irish Times* reported that, "The Commanding Officer of the 1st battalion, City of Dublin Cadets requests all cadets and ex-cadets of the force to parade in Wellington Barracks at 8 o'clock this evening with a view of enrolling for garrison duty or active service if necessary."

Within weeks, the regiments of the regular British Army had been deployed to the front in France and Belgium. The 1st Battalion of the East Surrey regiment, which had been stationed in Wellington, joined the 14th Brigade of the 5th Division of the British Expeditionary Force. The East Surreys landed

Recruiting posters for the First World War: 'Be one of the 300,000' – Wellington Barracks was a recruiting depot during the War.

'Your First duty is to play your part in ending the war', John Redmond, 1915.

(Courtesy of the National Library of Ireland)

at Le Havre and during the first few months of the war gained honours at Mons, Le Cateau, on the Marne and on the Aisne. By the end of the year, the British regulars had suffered horrific losses, such that in some units of 1,000 men only 30 remained neither killed nor wounded by the close of the year. This amounted to a casualty rate of over 90% among the original British Expeditionary Force that had been sent to France.

From the outset Lord Kitchener, the Minister for War in the British Cabinet, recognised that it would be a long war and called for a million volunteers. The response across the UK was immediate and men thronged the recruiting offices and barracks throughout Britain. Dublin was in a more complex situation than most cities in the United Kingdom, however. Ireland was in the midst of a deepening political crisis over the introduction of Home Rule. On July 26, just over a week before Britain's entry into the war, the Irish Volunteers had illegally landed rifles at Howth and in subsequent disturbances in Dublin city, British troops had shot dead three people and injured 37. Nevertheless, the troops such as the East Surreys who departed Dublin in August 1914 generally got a warm send-off. *The Irish Times* reported, "The scenes in Dublin during the embarkation cannot fail to have been cheering and encouraging to the gallant soldiers... From the early hours of the morning large crowds assembled on the quays to cheer the troops on their way and to wish them God-speed on their adventure. The main thoroughfares through which the troops passed were lined with spectators and on all sides indications were given of popular sympathy and goodwill."

Aided by the call of Irish Parliamentary Party Leader, John Redmond, for Irish nationalists to enlist in the military to fight for small nations and for Irish Home Rule, over 21,000 Dubliners joined up in the first two years of the war and 25,644 served in total from 1914-1918. Intensive recruitment efforts in Ireland continued throughout the war and while enlistment figures lagged somewhat behind Britain itself, some 130,000 men volunteered for military service.

Wellington Barracks was used a recruiting centre and training depot for troops being sent to France. However, by 1916 it was sparsely occupied by a garrison of about 100 men. Frank Laird, an Irishman serving in the British Army, described the barracks' population as, "about a hundred old crocks, who formed the nucleus of a garrison battalion".

The Easter Rising

Unknown to the barracks' garrison, just down the South Circular Road the 3rd Battalion of the Irish Volunteers Dublin Brigade was preparing for insurrection in April of that year. They assembled, on Easter Sunday, at nearby Emerald Square and proceeded to occupy South Dublin Union, now St James's Hospital, and other posts in the vicinity as part of the Easter Rising.

Two young Volunteers were sent to make sure that troops inside Wellington were not being mobilised against them. One of the Volunteers' scouts, Robert Holland, turned up at one of the Volunteers' posts at Marrowbone Lane, having forgotten to check the barracks. He recalled:

> [Volunteer officer Con] Colbert then took all my equipment from me and handed me a .38 nickel-plated revolver with about 20 rounds of ammunition. He says "What about your job on the barracks?" I told him it would take me two minutes from the South Circular Road entrance of Wellington Barracks to the Cork Street entrance of Ardee Street Brewery ... [He] said to go to the gate of Wellington Barracks and to watch the military and if I saw anything suspicious such as troops forming up on the Square or the filling up of cars with troops, and if anything like this occurred previous to 11.15 I was immediately to return to Emerald Square. If nothing occurred I was to stay there until two minutes to twelve and then proceed to Ardee Street Brewery. I proceeded to Wellington Barracks as directed and stayed there. Nothing abnormal occurred and I left two minutes to twelve and went to Ardee Street Brewery.

The other was Thomas Young, who was ordered to scout the area of the South Circular Road for troop movements:

> I was further ordered to take my party to a position where I could command a view of the gates of Wellington Barracks, so that I could prevent any troops in numbers leaving the Barracks. I was to maintain this position until twelve o'clock noon, when I could withdraw. I took up a position at the junction of Wellington St. and Wolsely Street where I had a fair view of the main gate of Wellington Barracks. No British military came out from the Barracks. I withdrew at twelve o'clock and returned to Emerald Square, but found no Volunteers there. I proceeded down Marrowbone Lane.

Easter Rising: the GPO in ruins. Inset: Con Colbert, the Volunteer officer, who ordered Wellington to be scouted on the outbreak of the Rising. (Courtesy of the National Library of Ireland)

In fact the troops in Wellington, even had they known that rebellion was breaking out, were in no position to do anything about it. Inside the barracks, the meagre garrison had initially just six rifles between them, their arms having for some reason been transferred elsewhere some nights before.

Frank Laird, an officer in the Dublin Fusiliers, was stationed in the Royal Barracks (subsequently Collins Barracks and now the National Museum) on the north side of the River Liffey but had been visiting family in Rathmines when the fighting broke out. Cycling back towards the Royal Barracks, he skirted around fighting taking place at the bridge over the Grand Canal near Portobello Barracks and was directed for his own safety by a British officer into Wellington. There he found the under strength and poorly armed garrison and "another hundred waifs and strays like myself, who had blown in".

One soldier suggested retiring to the upper floors of the barracks so that the rebels might leave them alone. Another complained that he had brought his wife and family to Dublin to escape German air raids, only to now find them in the middle of a rebellion. Fortunately for them, the complex was not attacked during the week's fighting and more arms were sent to Wellington in the following days.

A patrol dispatched from the barracks up towards Wexford Street was fired on, losing one dead and one wounded. Frank Laird recalled, "A ration party of a sergeant and three men... walked into a trap down some side street. Fire was opened on them suddenly from the houses and one man was shot through the head. Another man ran straight ahead and disappeared". He later, sheepishly, returned to the barracks in civilian clothes.

On the other side, a Volunteer named Seamus Kavanagh stationed in Jacob's biscuit factory heard that British troops were advancing along Camden Street, as if to launch an attack on Jacob's:

> When I had reported this information to the Countess Markievicz, Tom Donoghue and a Citizen Army man whose name I cannot remember, and myself were ordered to proceed along Cuffe Street. Just as we reached Fanning's, the chandlers, we saw the head of the British column at the Cuffe St. end of Wexford St. We lay down, and opened fire on them, wounding about three of them, whom I saw falling. They seemed to scatter in all directions. They were 6 British "Tommies" being marched along Wexford St. We fell back on the Green then. We expected them to come down Montague St. and attack us at Harcourt St., but we got word that they had returned to Wellington Barracks (now Griffith Barracks). They probably had been out scouting.

Another British officer in the barracks later accidentally shot himself in the leg. Wellington also came under sniper fire. According to Laird, "An industrious sniper took his station each evening about seven o'clock at the corner house up the road and did his best to pick off the sentry at the gate. A few barrels filled with earth frustrated this project but our friend persisted night after night for an hour or two". They raided the houses in the area but could not find the sniper.

According to Volunteer accounts, long range machine gun fire from the barracks was directed at the insurgent position at Jacob's biscuit factory, while according to Laird, at least one civilian, an unlucky rector of a nearby church who had climbed the steeple to watch the battle, was shot in the arm by a lieutenant. Some troops from Wellington manned a checkpoint at the Rialto Bridge over the Canal, where they arrested a number of Volunteers trying to join the rebel garrison at South Dublin Union.

It was not until the following Sunday, when the insurgents in South Dublin Union and Jacob's Factory had surrendered, that the garrison of Wellington could emerge safely from behind the walls of the barracks. Damage in the immediate area had been slight, but elsewhere much of central Dublin lay in ruins and up to 500 people, around half of them civilians, lay dead.

Losing rifles to the Volunteers 1917-18

Subsequently, as peaceful conditions returned to Dublin, the Barracks resumed its normal role.

However, by mid-1917, with the prisoners from the Rising already released, conflict was again in the air. The Irish Volunteers, soon to be called the Irish Republican Army or IRA, prepared for guerrilla warfare against British troops in the Irish capital by rearming, often at the expense of the armoury in Wellington Barracks. Even before the 1916 Rising, a young 3rd Battalion Volunteer named Joe Brophy, who was also employed as a telegraph messenger, stole and bought rifles off soldiers in Wellington.

The burnt out shell of the Linen Hall Barracks. Wellington was not directly attacked but was harassed by sniper fire during the Rising. (Courtesy of the National Library of Ireland)

On one occasion he even stole a pair of binoculars from a Major O'Hara at the barracks.

An IRA quartermaster named Kit Farrell, with the aid of a sympathetic Irish serviceman called Edward Handley, bought and smuggled over 100 rifles and thousands of rounds of ammunition out of the barracks – ferrying the weapons over the canal at the rear of the complex by night in small batches in late 1917 and early 1918.

Edward Handley was a Dublin Fusilier on leave from France, where he had been wounded, and stationed with the Labour Corps at Wellington Barracks, where he served as a storeman with access to the armoury. He got in touch with Farrell through a mutual friend in the Irish Citizen Army. Handley recalled:

> I was later transferred to a newly formed Labour Corps at Wellington Barracks where I was again able to pass out rifles at the back gate near Harold's Cross Bridge. A military policeman who had been transferred from Portobello with me knew what I was doing and was sympathetic. I always chose the time he was on duty at the back gate to pass out the rifles. In Wellington Barracks there were huts where men used to go for lectures on wet days. They often left their rifles outside the huts and it was an easy matter to take a few. As I was a storeman I did not attract undue attention when walking around with the

rifles. The men, of course, had to pay for the lost rifles and this generally seemed to satisfy the authorities, although there were periodical searches of traders vans here also. My military policeman friend always gave notice of any searches that were to take place.

He later played up his patriotic motives in helping to arm the Volunteers but it was also clear that he was well paid for his activities. According to Joseph O'Connor, an IRA officer in the 3rd Battalion:

> About this time, the Quartermaster, Christie Farrell, of "A" Company, got in touch with some British soldiers stationed in Wellington Barracks, what is now known as Griffith Barracks. They were willing to hand over rifles and ammunition on the payment of a very small sum per rifle and per packet of ammunition, each packet containing fifty rounds; the price in either case never exceeded £1.

> This was a very valuable source of supply to us and we succeeded in getting up to 100 rifles and probably 1,000 rounds of ammunition before the discovery was made. The procedure adopted was, and this in the depth of winter, that our men should swim the canal from Parnell Road to the iron railings surrounding Wellington Barracks.

Christie 'Kit' Farrell, the quartermaster, left the most detailed account of the operation:

> The Grand Canal forms the rear boundary of the barracks which is situated between the bridges - Harold's Cross and Sally's Bridge. Inside barrack railings, at a point almost opposite to Greenmount Lane (on the opposite side of the canal) is a small red-bricked house known as the Schoolmaster's House. This house offered cover to both myself and the contact on the inside. It was decided that I would swim across the canal at this point. The rifles were to be passed out under the bottom bar of the railings. Time - 1 o'clock - striking by clock in the barrack tower. Signal – three low whistles.

> Next morning at 00.50 hours, seven men arrived at Greenmount Lane. Each man knew his job; everything in the vicinity was normal. Gas lamps bordering the road were dimmed by men detailed for that job. I swam across the canal. From my position on the canal bank I could see the light shining from the Guardroom and hear the measured tread of the sentry across the barrack square. As the barrack clock struck the hour, I gave the signal and received the answer and was in possession of three rifles. The Operation was definitely on. I strapped the rifles on my back, using the slings, and swam back to the boys. I was helped out. Very shortly the rifles were on their way to the dump at Jimmie Murray's home.

> I made about 14 crossings on different nights on this plan, out of which we obtained about 50 rifles. It was winter and on several occasions I swam through a thin coating of ice. On one occasion I was about half-way across when I received the danger signal. I had four rifles strapped on my back and had to remain longer than usual in the water. I was seized with cramp and was taken from the water by Peadar O'Meara. The cause of the danger signal was a couple of soldiers who, accompanied by their lady friends, arrived at the spot where I had intended to land. They would select that spot to say goodnight. They were soon got rid of by Jimmie Murray who proceeded to mend an imaginary puncture in the wheel of his cycle. We now received our first setback. Our inside contact was suspicious of things inside and requested us to lay off until we heard from him.

Wellington Barracks from the canal c.1900. (Courtesy of the National Library of Ireland)

During the waiting period we decided to change our plan and work from the front of the barracks. About a week elapsed before we received the all clear from the soldiers. I explained the change of plan to our contact. He pointed out the fact that, though it was a quicker means of getting the rifles away, it exposed to greater danger the men working on the outside as they would be practically in full view of the sentry and could be seen quite easily. The risk was ours. We took it.

The main entrance to Wellington Barracks was on the South Circular Road. Inside the gate was situated the guardroom and a sentry post. About 50 yards from this post towards Leonard's Corner is another gate which is more or less covered by the shadow of a block of buildings facing the road. It was through this gate we proposed the rifles should be passed to us. Our first attempt here was so successful that we carried on at intervals for about six weeks. In spite of the close proximity of the sentry, rifles were passed through the bars of the gate, carried across the road and dispatched to the dump. Very shortly, and very unfortunate for us, this regiment was transferred elsewhere. The entire operation gave us over 100 rifles and some ammunition.

It says much about the laxity of security in the barracks at the time that not only was Handley not caught and punished, he was subsequently transferred as storeman to military posts at the North Wall, near Dublin Port and Kingstown (now Dun Laoghaire) where he clandestinely supplied more arms from embarking and disembarking soldiers to his contact in the Citizen Army.

However, the incident meant that, according to a member of the Leinster Regiment: "command decided they couldn't trust the Irish regiments. They brought over an English regiment to replace each Irish unit and we were put back on the boats that they came over on".

A civilian, or IRA member, killed after the IRA raid on the Customs House in May 1921. (Courtesy of the National Library of Ireland)

During the War of Independence

In November 1918, Wellington Barracks hosted a military display for the children of the Liberties to celebrate the end of the First World War. However, just over a month later the Sinn Fein party swept the boards in the Irish General Election, pledging not only to renounce Irish participation in the British military, but to break the connection completely between Britain and Ireland. They declared an Irish Republic and their parliament, the Dáil, met in Dublin for the first time in January 1919.

British efforts to suppress this republic and the parallel attempts of the IRA to hamstring the British administration led gradually to a situation of guerrilla warfare which we now call the Irish War of Independence. In Dublin until late 1920, this mainly consisted of assassinations of selected British Army and Dublin Metropolitan Police intelligence operatives by a select IRA unit named the Squad under Michael Collins – most famously on Bloody Sunday in November 1920, when they killed fourteen British soldiers and policemen in one night. However, from late 1920, the Volunteer or IRA Battalions in the city were also instructed to form Active Service Units or ASUs and to attack British troops in the streets.

From early 1921 to July of that year, the garrison at Wellington was harassed by small scale guerrilla attacks by the ASU of the Dublin IRA 3rd Battalion while on their patrols. Typically the IRA men used revolvers and grenades, which were easy to conceal and could be used in cramped urban conditions. During this time, Wellington was garrisoned by the 1st Battalion of the Prince of Wales' Volunteers and then by a battalion of the South Lancashire regiment.

IRA statements record at least three ambushes of patrols from Wellington in the immediate vicinity of the barracks. Joseph McGuiness, one of the ASU fighters recalled:

> *Early in March, 1921, the section staged an ambush on a British foot patrol of about twenty-five men who were patrolling the area from Inchicore via Rialto Bridge to Wellington Barracks, South Circular Road.*

> We took up a position in a field near Rialto Bridge, which was the property of Alderman Flanagan. We lay behind a stone wall and waited until the patrol came into view and within revolver range.
>
> Jimmy McGuinness was in charge and he ordered us to open fire on them, which we did. Evidently the party were taken completely by surprise as they seemed to run amok and did not return the fire. I cannot say if we caused any casualties amongst them.

Another 3rd Battalion IRA guerrilla, Padraig O'Connor, was involved in ambushing a car load of intelligence officers (known to the IRA as the 'Igoe Gang') in Dolphin's Barn on their way to Wellington Barracks on June 30, 1921. Ten IRA men fired on the car in the square in Dolphin's Barn. O'Connor recalled:

> One officer in the back was returning the fire all the time. Our party at the Laundry opened fire on the car when it came abreast of their position, but the driver brought the car to Wellington Barracks. Most of the occupants of the car were either killed or wounded. The return fire from the car wounded one civilian who was passing at the time. Our party got away safely.

'Good Bye Dublin': British troops prepare to be shipped out of Dublin. (Courtesy of the National Library of Ireland)

There were further ambushes of troops from the barracks on the South Circular Road and Harold's Cross, though the attackers were not sure if any casualties had been caused.

Not far from Wellington Barracks, the Wexford Street/ Camden Street/ Aungier Street/ George's Street thoroughfare became known as the 'Dardanelles' (after the 1915 campaign in the First World War), such was the frequency of IRA gun and grenade attacks on British troops passing to and from the city centre to the barracks at Portobello and Wellington. The ambushes, mostly carried out by Volunteers from the 3rd Battalion, were a danger to civilians as well as British personnel, killing at least two. On 16 March 1921, a troop lorry from Wellington barracks, carrying soldiers from the South Lancashire Regiment, was hit by two grenades hurled from overlooking buildings on Wexford Street, killing two of the British soldiers, Lance Corporal Jarvis and Private G. Thomas and wounding six, one of whom, Private Whiting, died from his wounds two days later.

The War of Independence did not see any large scale military actions in Dublin, but did see some 300 people lose their lives in the city and over 4,000 arrested. The IRA could never attempt to drive the British troops from barracks such as Wellington. Rather, their strategy was to continually harass them and therefore to apply further pressure for a political settlement.

To an extent this succeeded. Under the terms of the Anglo-Irish Treaty, signed on 6 December 1921, the British military were to evacuate all their posts in the southern 26 counties of Ireland and to hand them over to the newly created Irish Free State. The period of British military use of Wellington Barracks was coming to an end.

The building pictured in this watercolour by Aidan Powell was the barracks' medical centre. It was later used by the Revenue Commissioners to store tax files.

Chapter 3
Griffith Barracks in the Irish Civil War 1922-23

Free State officers in front of armoured cars. Centre in the front row is Tom Ennis, who commanded the National Army takeover of Wellington Barracks.

(Courtesy of the National Library of Ireland)

The Irish Times reported on 12 April 1922: "At 8 o'clock this morning, Wellington barracks Dublin was taken over by official IRA troops of the 2nd Eastern Division under Commandant T. [Tom] Ennis." The *Times* noted: "There was a complete absence of ceremonial and the formal handing over of the barracks [by the British Army] attracted little attention".

Under the terms of the Anglo-Irish Treaty, British troops were being evacuated from the territory of the new Irish Free State – the handover process began in January 1922 with the handing over of Beggars Bush barracks in Dublin, but did not get underway in earnest until April of that year. With all the experience of moving posts across a far flung empire, the British troops moved to their port of embarkation swiftly and smoothly. Michael Collins was anxious for the British to hand over barracks and arms to his new Irish administration. Neville Macready, British Commander in Chief, was happy to hand over Wellington, which by that time was almost empty.

However, the takeover of barracks in general and Wellington in particular was no straightforward task, for there were by now two antagonistic Irish armed forces on the ground. One of them, loyal to the Provisional Government set up under the Treaty, was to be called the National Army but in April 1922 when elements of its 1st Eastern Division occupied Wellington Barracks, was still calling itself the 'official IRA'.

The other was that element of the IRA which rejected the Treaty and its disestablishment of the Irish Republic declared in 1919. They termed themselves simply the Irish Republican Army, or Republicans, but were called by their pro-Treaty opponents the 'Irregulars' or 'Mutineers'. The split between former comrades in the IRA over the Treaty was deeply bitter and personal, a fact illustrated nowhere better than in the 3rd Dublin Battalion, based in the south west of the city – the area around Wellington Barracks. For Padraig O'Connor, for instance, a guerrilla fighter in 3rd Battalion's active service unit in the fight against the British, the endorsement of the Treaty by his chief, Michael Collins, was recommendation enough. He joined the first unit of the National Army, the Dublin Guard, which paraded in Beggars Bush Barracks, some three kilometres along the Grand Canal from Wellington, in February 1922.

For Joseph O'Connor (no relation), on the other hand, the commander of the IRA's 3rd Dublin Battalion, the Treaty was a betrayal: "I felt that it was wrong to accept any settlement with England for less than the absolute freedom of our whole country. Now that the Dáil had accepted the new position I deemed that they had exceeded their powers, and that it was my duty to continue striving until England withdrew all her forces and we had complete control of our affairs". He led much of the battalion into opposition to the Treaty and the Provisional Government in March 1922 when he endorsed a decision of the IRA Executive to disavow the authority of the Dáil, which had passed the Treaty.

For this reason, the occupation of barracks across the country in the spring of 1922 became a race between the two sides. At Wellington in particular, Jim Harpur, an officer in the National Army

British troops being replaced by National Army troops at Richmond Barracks in 1922. Similar scenes took place at Wellington Barracks in April 1922. (Courtesy of the National Library of Ireland)

stationed at Beggars Bush, was told by Tom Ennis, "that Irregular elements were contemplating having the barracks handed over to them. He instructed me to get a company together and proceed to Wellington Barracks at 0800 hours. He undertook to inform the British O/C". The next morning when the Irish troops marched into the barracks, the British officer commanding duly presented arms, showed Harpur around the barracks and marched his men out with the band playing. This, however, was only the start of the new garrison's problems.

The new garrison of the barracks

The barracks was the depot of the Free State's Eastern Command under Dan Hogan, a former IRA commander from Monaghan. It also, from September 1922, housed the Army's Intelligence Department under Charles Dalton, brother of Emmet, one of the National Army's senior commanders. Both Daltons had worked closely with Michael Collins and his 'Squad' in the struggle against the British. Charles had worked as an intelligence officer and occasionally a gunman too. Several members of his intelligence unit in Wellington Barracks – such as Joe Dolan and Frank Bolster – had been assassins in the Squad and were to carry their efficiency at killing into the internecine conflict that followed the Treaty.

The National Army Intelligence Department was the heir of Michael Collins's GHQ intelligence organisation of 1919-1921. A new intelligence organisation was established right after the truce with the British in July 1921. Liam Tobin, who had been under Collins in GHQ intelligence was made the new Director of Intelligence, based at Portobello Barracks. In early August 1922, this organisation evolved into the CID (Criminal Investigation Department), based in Oriel House – a plain clothes, armed, detective unit. In September 1922, Joe McGrath TD was put in charge of the CID (whose operational head was Pat Moynihan) and Tobin was re-assigned to a new Army Intelligence Department. Charles Dalton was made head Intelligence Officer in Dublin, based in Wellington Barracks. The job of the Intelligence Department was to gather information, launch raids on republican safe houses and arrest and interrogate suspects. They soon developed a ferocious reputation. Frank Sherwin, a fighter with the anti-Treatyites wrote: "The Intelligence Officers were a law unto themselves. They were usually drunk and trigger happy. Wellington Barracks was the worst."

The regular garrison of Wellington was also tasked with general patrolling in Dublin city, to guard against anti-Treaty IRA attacks and also to maintain civil order.

Free State or National Army soldiers parade in Wellington Barracks, in front of the guardhouse in 1922.
(Courtesy of the National Library of Ireland)

Recruits for the National Army enter Wellington Barracks, 1922. (Courtesy of the National Library of Ireland)

Wellington Barracks was also a training depot where new recruits were knocked into shape before being sent to areas of guerrilla activity elsewhere in the country. Most of the NCOs who were in charge of this training seem to have been veterans of the British Army and of the First World War. An orderly sergeant at an inquest in November 1922, for instance, spoke with an English accent, though he defensively maintained he was an Irishman and said he "was no stranger to machine gun fire" – indicating he had served in the Great War.

The vast bulk of recruits, however were veterans neither of the British Army nor the IRA. Some were as young as 16 or 17, recruited for a job, regular wages, meals and a place to live. The overwhelming majority of them were from Dublin's working class inner city. The military census of November 1922 recorded 644 officers and men in Wellington Barracks. One page of the census entry for Wellington gives us an idea of the profile of the National Army soldiers there. Out of nine infantry soldiers listed, seven were from Dublin city or county. Five were listed as 18 or 19 years old, but may in fact have been younger, and the oldest was 23.

One of the tragedies of the period was that Wellington Barracks, with its garrison of very young and mostly inexperienced soldiers, saw considerably more violence during the Civil War than it had in the preceding War of Independence.

First attacks

Even in April 1922, with the official start of the civil war still months away, things were far from peaceful. Within days of taking over the barracks, the garrison at Griffith was attacked twice by anti-Treaty IRA fighters. An Army statement of April 19, 1922 stated: "men dressed in civilian clothes came up to the gate and fired point blank at the men in the square". Two men were wounded. The attackers, two men carrying automatic pistols, sped away by car, only to be stopped at a roadblock and arrested.

Two days later on April 21, another, more determined attack was made. It was 11.20pm and the troops were under curfew. Only the sentries at the gates of the barracks were still up. Suddenly fire opened from the rooftops all around the barracks. The sentries scrambled for cover behind a steam roller and bullets pinged off the granite bricks. For an hour, the two sides exchanged fire. Two attackers tried to rush the front gate, throwing grenades at the soldiers inside. They replied with bombs of their own. A total of five men were wounded in the skirmish.

The context of these attacks was the occupation, by anti-Treaty IRA forces, of the Four Courts in defiance of the Provisional Government. Attacks were also made in these days on government buildings, Beggars Bush Barracks and the Bank of Ireland headquarters on College Green. Although

Artillery outside the Four Courts. (Courtesy of the National Library of Ireland)

Civil War in Dublin – troops at Nelson's Pillar. (Courtesy of the National Library of Ireland)

Rory O'Connor, IRA commander in the Four Courts, denied responsibility for the shootings, this seems unconvincing.

While in the following months, Michael Collins, head of the Provisional Government, made strenuous efforts to re-unite the republican movement, it was clear that at some point that the government would have to assert its authority or the Free State would collapse, bringing with it the possibility of British re-occupation.

Civil War

On June 28, 1922, the undeclared civil war became official when Free State troops opened fire with artillery on the anti-Treaty forces in the Four Courts. The fighting in Dublin was over within a week, with pro-Treaty troops securing the capital. Within a month, the original garrison of Wellington was sent to different parts of the country to break up anti-Treaty resistance, principally to Counties Wexford, Cork and Kerry. By the end of August, the main towns and cities had all been occupied by Free State forces but a new phase of the war was about to begin, as the anti-Treaty IRA embarked on a campaign of guerrilla warfare in the hope of bringing down the Free State.

The victory of the pro-Treaty forces in the fighting of the summer of 1922 came at a terrible cost, taking the lives of Arthur Griffith, President of the Second Dáil (who died of a stroke) and Michael Collins, National Army Commander in Chief, who was killed in an ambush in County Cork. Later that year Wellington Barracks was renamed Griffith Barracks in honour of Arthur Griffith.

Soon the grim ritual of military funerals for members of the garrison killed in action became a familiar sight in the barracks. Michael Crampton, for example, was only 17 when joined the Army, and was a native of Church Street in the Liberties. He died in Wexford on 25 July, killed in an ambush while escorting a train. Another Volunteer, a man named Cuddell, a driver attached to motor transport in Wellington Barracks, was killed near Fermoy in Cork, with two other soldiers. A mine blew the Crossley tender he was driving "to fragments" and "the right side of his face was almost blown away".

In Dublin itself, the garrison of the barracks found themselves policing a restive population, without training or guidance. Some died in accidents, the result of mixing so many inexperienced youths with loaded weapons. One such was Francis Denham (18), who was mistakenly shot by another Free State soldier while on guard duty at Harcourt Street train station. Another boy soldier, Sean Sullivan, a sergeant major at only 16 years and 10 months, died in a scuffle while trying to clear a street outside a pub in the north inner city. His commanding officer fired a shot over the heads of a crowd, only for it to ricochet back off a roof and kill young Sullivan.

All this time, menacing the raw, nervy young men, was the threat of attack, mostly by the IRA 3rd Dublin Battalion, former comrades of some of the garrison. The troops in Wellington were regularly ambushed with a sudden volley of shots, or a grenade thrown at a passing troop lorry. In one incident, a lorry heading back into Wellington barracks was ambushed at Curzon Street, across the South Circular Road. A grenade flew through the air, only to miss the troops and land in Williams' newsagents. Maureen Carroll, a girl of only seven and another man, were seriously injured in the ensuing

The YMCA and other buildings on fire.
(Courtesy of the National Library of Ireland)

Buildings burning at the north end of O'Connell Street, July 1922. (Courtesy of the National Library of Ireland)

fire fight. The soldiers bundled out of their lorry and chased the ambushers down the maze of red brick streets. They caught them on Kevin Street. The troops claimed that the two, Sean McEvoy and John Hardwood, tried to "bolt". Both men were shot, and McEvoy killed. The barracks was also harassed by sniper fire on a nightly basis. On one occasion this resulted in a passerby being killed. Margaret King, an 18 year old draper's assistant, was shot dead by an unseen sniper while walking home past the barracks.

The activities of the republicans were, however, generally minor in scale, often involving destruction of roads and communications rather than direct attacks on troops. On September 16, 1922, for example, troops from Wellington Barracks found men dismantling nearby Rialto Bridge with pickaxes and spades, who fled when fired on. This disruption of everyday life does not appear to have been popular in Dublin. One anti-Treaty guerrilla, Frank Sherwin, remembered, "most of the people were against us in the civil war".

Prisoners

Combating the republican guerrillas meant finding out who they were, where their safe-houses were located and then arresting or killing them. This was primarily the job of Charlie Dalton's Intelligence Department. His men, along with regular troops from the barracks, raided known republican safe houses and arrested hundreds of suspects.

By September 1922, 140 prisoners were held behind barbed wire in the barracks. By November, the number was over 250. In the Dáil, on September 13, 1922, George Gavan Duffy questioned the Minister for Home Affairs, Kevin O'Higgins about why one particular prisoner "Dr. Bastable, of Glasgow, was arrested on the 8th instant and imprisoned in Wellington Barracks; by whose authority, for what reason, and on what charge Dr. Bastable has been arrested; and whether the application of his solicitor, Mr. John Cusack, to visit him on professional business will be acceded to". O'Higgins responded simply that, "Prisoners arrested in an area in which hostilities are not definitely ended must be regarded as military prisoners in the war zone" and that he had no information about the man in question.

Prisoners were first taken on entry to the barracks to the guard room and then deposited either in cells or in the barracks gym. Joseph O'Connor, the commander of the anti-Treaty IRA's 3rd Dublin Battalion was captured in late October 1922: "After some days in the guardroom where were also Pat Sweeney, Michael Price and the four men captured at Oriel House, I was sent to the gymnasium, which had been wired off and made into a collecting cage". He describes the conditions in the gym: "The conditions in the Gym were awful, particularly in the mornings after the place had been locked up for twelve hours. The doctors when appealed to, stated the place should house fifty men and not more".

Wellington was a holding centre rather than a prison and the typical stay of prisoners there was 7-8 weeks. O'Connor was moved to the much larger internment camp, nicknamed 'Tintown' in the Curragh just before Christmas 1922 and was held there until 1924.

Kevin O'Higgins, Minister for Home Affairs.
(Courtesy of the National Library of Ireland)

48 GRIFFITH BARRACKS IN THE IRISH CIVIL WAR 1922-23

Another prisoner at Wellington in September 1922 was a lawyer, Dermot Crowley, who was arrested by intelligence officers after he had filed a writ of habeas corpus demanding the release of republican prisoners. He wrote to his friend and former colleague, Cahir Davitt, the new Attorney General of the Irish Free State:

> *From what I have since seen and heard I believe he is one of the body called 'Intelligence Officers' – a body specially created by Mr. [Richard] Mulcahy since he-became Minister for Defence, and apparently trained after the methods practised by the British Auxiliaries in this country, but with a great deal more coarseness and savagery than the Auxiliaries were capable of. On arrival here he searched my pockets and took my cheque book, some private letters I had, and a pocket book containing various things. I have got back none of these.*
>
> *I have since been locked up in a filthy cell and have never undressed at night – Thursday to Monday – the two so-called blankets supplied being unclean. The dimensions of the cell are about nine feet long, seven wide, and ten in height. The following night (Friday) another person was put in with me.*
>
> *On Saturday there were five, and last night (Sunday) nine of us in this cell. We have been locked up here day and night except for fifteen or twenty minutes exercise each day in the yard. I have scarcely eaten anything since my arrival. The food given to the prisoners in these cells consists of the leavings of the common soldiers in the guardroom adjoining, who never use a knife or fork themselves.*

Disturbing stories soon emerged of the treatment the prisoners in Wellington received. Anti-Treaty commander Ernie O'Malley wrote a letter to the newspapers complaining that "Commandants Dan Coughlan and Frank Bolster" had "kicked prisoners senseless" at Wellington Barracks. On Saturday September 30th, an urgent request was sent to nearby Mount Argus Church for a priest to see a prisoner, Fergus Murphy. He had been wounded in the head. The priest, Fr. Kieran Farrelly, raced to the barracks, but troops there told him: "it's nothing, a minor scalp wound". Unconvinced, he went looking for Murphy among the prisoners. Standing at the barbed wire, he found him:

> *As he drew near, I had a sickening feeling, because I had never before seen a man after torture. His head, from the eyes and ears upwards, was heavily bandaged. His eyes were blacked and twitching with pain. His face on both sides of the nose was also black. His right cheek was terribly swollen. I asked him what had happened him. He motioned to the Intelligence Department and said, "They took me down there last night and left me as you see me".*

On October 4, T.J. O'Connell TD asked W.T. Cosgrave, now President of the Dáil, about the allegations of mistreatment of prisoners in Wellington and Fergus Murphy in particular: "It is a matter of common knowledge to this Dáil that widespread complaints have been made with regard to the treatment of prisoners". Cosgrave responded that the medical officer at Wellington had stated that "'this man came into the barracks suffering from old wounds. There are no prisoners in the barracks suffering from the effects of ill-treatment. Now an investigation is taking place in this case, and disciplinary action will be taken if any charge is proved".

Dermot Crowley wrote to Cahir Davitt at around the same time telling of the beating of prisoners:

> Some of the occupants of this cell and the adjoining one have been frequently interrogated concerning themselves and other people and savagely assaulted. This is done by the 'Intelligence Officers' referred to. I have witnessed instances of it. Once when I was being interrogated myself another officer intervened and said: "This is a special case".
>
> On three separate occasions that night the cell door was opened and the prisoner dragged out and savagely beaten because he could not or would not give information about other people. On the third occasion an order was given outside to a number of soldiers to form a firing party and to load. I heard these orders and the actual loading of the rifles. I heard other appalling expressions likewise. My soul sickened at the thought that I belonged to a country where such abominations were committed and paid for by the people.
>
> The prisoner seemed to have been taken out into the yard out of hearing, and about half an hour passed. Then he was brought back by a different officer who remarked: "Only for me you would have gone west that time!" The next day in my presence the same prisoner, was subjected to another "interrogation". A revolver was put to his face and he was told three times that he would be taken out that night at 12.30 and shot. Two hours later he was taken to an office for further "interrogation". I was standing at the door of that office. I heard his moans of pain inside. He came out with his face swollen at both sides. He said some of his teeth were broken.
>
> An officer accompanied us back to our cell. He seemed sorry for the continued persecution of this man. I told him of the threat to take the prisoner out that night and shoot him, and asked who was in charge of the barrack, and why these "Intelligence Officers" were allowed to come in at all hours of the night to practise such infamies. This officer said: "I am in charge of the barrack, and this man will not be shot to-night". He added: "But he was lucky in not being shot as soon as he was arrested".

Crowley, who was not a member of the IRA, eventually went on hunger strike and was released in October 1922.

The Dirty War

The officer quoted by Crowley who feared that prisoners were being shot out of hand by the Intelligence Department was not worrying unnecessarily. On October 6, 1922, Charles Dalton arrested three youths in Drumcondra who had been putting up republican posters and brought them to the barracks for questioning. They were interrogated by officers there and then discharged. The following day their bodies were found at the Red Cow in Clondalkin, shot in the head. Edwin Hughes and Brendan Holohan were 17. Their friend, Joseph Rogers, was a year younger.

An inquest was held the following month and the prosecution counsel asked for a verdict of murder to be brought against Dalton. The jury, perhaps afraid of crossing the army, declined. In fact, Dalton was put under arrest by the CID, a police counter-insurgency unit largely made up of former IRA men, with an equally grim record as the Army Intelligence Department, but was never charged.

There were complaints from their own side that the intelligence officers were too wedded to raids rather than intelligence gathering. One intelligence officer, Bryan, complained that they sat around the office in Wellington waiting for a tip-off so that they could raid, rather than analysing intelligence. Nevertheless, the Intelligence Department could be effective. They had extensive knowledge of how the IRA worked in Dublin and other information was, quite simply, battered out of their prisoners. On November 4, 1922, they captured Ernie O'Malley, commander of the anti-Treaty IRA's Eastern Division, in a raid on his safe-house on Aylesbury Road.

The attack on Wellington Barracks, 8 November 1922

Early on the morning of November 8, 1922, the republicans made their most determined attack on Wellington Barracks during the Civil War. The attack seems to have been part of a general 'hit-up' by the republicans in the city. The other military barracks around the city were also attacked in the same week.

The barracks' orderly clerk was attending the morning parade where the soldiers, mostly unarmed, were listening to the order of the day read by the regimental sergeant major, when he heard machine gun fire. The clerk at first thought it was practice firing. Then he saw spurts of dust spring up from the ground as the bullets landed around him and flung himself to the ground. Another soldier told *The Irish Times*: "I will not forget this morning for some time to come. It was a pretty tight corner to be in. The first outburst crashed in on us just like a flash of lightning, and did most of the damage. All of us that could crawled around for cover, it was simply death to walk in the square at that time".

The republicans had occupied the upper stories and roofs of the houses across the canal, at the back of the barracks. From there, they raked the parade square with rifle and machine gun fire. The sound was deafening to the stricken soldiers. One said: "It seemed as if marbles were being rained down from an immense height". A total of eighteen soldiers were hit. One was killed instantly and seventeen badly injured. As the firing started, a butchers van owned by one R. McGurk of Harolds Cross was making a delivery to the barracks. The storm of bullets peppered the unfortunate delivery men, killing their horse and mortally wounding the driver. According to a soldier on the scene "the whole thing lasted about 15 minutes, the rest of the soldiers came out then and started some Lewis guns going."

One hundred soldiers had been lined up on the square shoulder to shoulder. Given that a large number of republicans had been involved in the attack, that they had time to set up their targets, which were around 50 metres away, and given that they were armed with Lee Enfield rifles and Thompson and Lewis machine guns, it says something about the poor marksmanship of the attackers that more soldiers were not killed. The republicans made their escape across country, through the villages of Kimmage and Crumlin, pursued by Free State troops. They were seen carrying two badly wounded men of their own. The army later claimed the two were killed in the fire-fight

Reprisals for the attack

Free State troops flooded the area around Wellington Barracks after the attack and ambulances dashed to and from the hospital with the casualties. Most of the attackers had got away. But in the aftermath of the attack, the Free State soldiers managed to exact some revenge for the attack. Inside the barracks, some soldiers opened fire on the prisoners locked inside the gym. Joseph O'Connor recalled:

> Whilst there an attack on the barracks took place. It was a good sharp fight, but when it was ended our turn came. We were crowded into the Gymnasium and the door locked. Some [Free] Staters got outside the north door with sub-machine guns and fired through the wooden door, but "God directs the bullets". A strong inside iron bolt deflected the bullets. Only for this the casualties amongst the 250 prisoners would have been very great, but as it was, not more than half a dozen were wounded. Seán Forde was the prisoners' commandant, and handled the situation well. Pat Sweeney was one of those hit. This was the most brutal and cowardly act that I ever knew Irishmen to be guilty of.

James Spain, an anti-Treaty fighter who had been wounded in the leg while attacking the barracks, was spotted in the neighbouring streets trying to find a friendly house. A Mrs Doleman, of 22 Donore Road, was feeding her chickens, when a young man approached her, wounded in the leg, saying, "For God's sake let me in! Jesus Mary and Joseph help me, if they get me they'll shoot me!" She let him in, but hot on his heels was a Lancia armoured car with five soldiers in it. They pulled him out of the house. His body was dumped in nearby Susan Street, shot five times in the chest and head.

In sweeps of the immediate area, the Free State troops picked up another twenty or so Republican suspects. Among them was Frank Sherwin, a member of the Fianna or IRA youth wing, who was arrested with arms along with five other youthful guerrillas who had been carrying out attacks in Dublin, but not, apparently, the one on Wellington Barracks. Sherwin remembered: "We were marched to Wellington Barracks, about a mile away. Some of the people on the street shouted and jeered at us. Perhaps they knew some of the soldiers who had been shot that morning". He was brought into the office of the Intelligence Department into the custody of Joe Dolan, one of Charles Dalton's men. He has left one of the most vivid accounts of the torture of prisoners. Dolan wanted to get the name of his commanding officer in the Fianna, Charles O'Connor. Sherwin refused to give it, fearing that if he did O'Connor would be killed. Dolan began to beat him: "My clothes were dragged off me until I was naked… I was lashed for about twenty minutes".

The following day they tried again. They hit him in the head with a revolver and poked him with wire. Dolan jabbed him with a bayonet and stuck a rifle into his mouth. He even produced a razor and threatened to cut the prisoner's throat. In the end they decided he wouldn't talk and threw him back in with the other prisoners. Sherwin recalled: "My face was swollen, my nose was broken, several teeth

Crowds gather outside the barracks after the attack. (Courtesy of the National Library of Ireland)

were missing and I had cuts and lumps on my head, with bruises all over my body. I could not stand or move for nine days". He was never to fully recover the use of his right arm.

The end of the Civil War

In terms of casualties inflicted, both killed and wounded, the eighteen Free State soldiers hit in the attack on Wellington on November 8, represented the high point for the anti-Treaty guerrilla campaign in Dublin. Two days later there were simultaneous, 20 minute attacks on both Wellington and Portobello barracks, including an attempt to kill National Army commander Richard Mulcahy, who lived inside the Portobello complex. Two civilians and one IRA man were killed in the attack on Portobello. A soldier was shot in the head but survived.

On November 24, there was another 'ineffective' sniping attack on Wellington that caused no casualties. In the New Year, on March 29 and May 26, 1923, the republican night attacks put some more bullet holes in the walls of the barracks but failed to hit anyone. Two more sentries at the barracks were also shot and killed at close range in separate incidents in March 1923, in what can only be described as assassinations. The anti-Treaty IRA also tried to assassinate Frank Bolster (one of the intelligence officers with a bad reputation) at the theatre in March 1923, shooting him but not killing him. For their part, intelligence officers from the garrison shot a civilian, Hugh Haughton, on Donore Avenue in March 1923, for having on him a copy of an IRA order to kill TDs.

However, compared to the initial months of the war, casualties in Dublin had dropped steeply – an indication that the republicans' campaign in the city was petering out. The anti-Treaty side officially called off their campaign in May 1923.

The Intelligence Department in Wellington Barracks did not outlast the Civil War. Both Liam Tobin and Charles Dalton were sidelined in a National Army reorganisation of early 1923. Tobin was made aide de camp of the Governor General and Dalton was made adjutant of the air service. They complained afterwards about being kept away from intelligence work. For this reason Dalton and Tobin were leaders of an attempted mutiny in March 1924 for which they were forced to resign from the Army.

Wellington was renamed Griffith Barracks in late 1922 after Arthur Griffith, the first President of the Executive Council of the Free State, who had died of a stroke during the Civil War in August 1922. The Civil War was perhaps the darkest chapter of the barracks' history. Much blood had been spilt and much suffering caused there, on both sides. Griffith Barracks, as it was now called, looked uneasily into its future in an independent Ireland.

Chapter 4
Griffith Barracks 1923-1991

View of bomb damage on the South Circular Road, January 1941, taken from behind the Griffith Barracks' railings.
(Courtesy of the National Library of Ireland)

Griffith Barracks emerged from the trauma of the Civil War into a peacetime role as a garrison for the much reduced Irish Army.

The Aftermath of the Civil War and the 1930s

In the wake of the Civil War, one of the first tasks facing the new government of the Irish Free State was to cut the size of its army. Out of a total government expenditure in 1923-24 of about £30 million, £10.5 million was spent on the National Army. From a high of 58,000 men during the Civil War, consuming some 30% of the new state's expenditure, it was reduced to 14,000 men in 1924, and by the 1930s was down to fewer than 10,000.

At Griffith Barracks, some special corps, which had been formed for the specific demands of the Civil War, were disbanded. One such unit was the Railway Protection, Repair and Maintenance Corps, which was charged with keeping the railways running amid the republican sabotage campaign. They moved into Griffith on January 12, 1923 and, their work completed, were disbanded in September 1923. The Intelligence Department, which had such a bad reputation during the Civil War was absorbed into a smaller, more specialised military intelligence section nicknamed the Second Bureau (later G2).

The Irish Army parades in 1933 for the Papal Nuncio's visit. (Courtesy of the National Library of Ireland)

By November 1923, such was the peaceful mood prevailing at Griffith that the Army journal *An tÓglach* devoted an extensive report to 'Hallwe'en at Griffith Barracks'. There was, it reported, "a very successful Military Boxing Tournament followed by a highly enjoyable concert". It continued, "Early in the day, many hands were involved, under the capable supervision of Comdt. Farrelly in decorating the spacious Recreation Hall". In 1924, *The Irish Times* reported on the visit of the National Army chess team to the barracks. There does appear to have been a small scandal at Griffith in 1924, however, when a commandant, Patrick Geraghty, was charged at the Dublin District Court with the embezzlement of £292 belonging to the laundry fund at Griffith Barracks.

Belongings loaded on a cart, the South Circular Road, January 1941.
(Courtesy of the National Library of Ireland)

Still, It was a far cry from November 1922, when the barracks was full of prisoners and bullets had rained down one morning on recruits at morning parade.

With the Army reduced in size after the Civil War, parts of the complex fell out of military use. Part of the parade ground was purchased by the Irish Amateur Boxing Association in 1937 (headed by former National Army general W.R.E. Murphy) and made into what is now the National Stadium.

Other parts were leased out into private hands. In September 1924, the barracks' married quarters was rented to Greenmount and Boyne Linen Company of Harold's Cross, who housed the families of their workers there. Four blocks of the barracks were used, comprising 40 flats of 3-4 rooms each, complete with running water and electricity. While the same blocks would in later decades become by-words for the worst type of slum housing in Dublin, in 1924, with over 25,000 families in the city living in one-room tenements, with no running water or electricity, the accommodation for the workers of Greenmount and Boyne must have seemed relatively good.

In the inter-war years, the Irish Army's garrison at Griffith was joined by the Army Corps of Engineers.

The Emergency

In 1938, with the clouds of war looming on the European mainland, a joint Army-Garda gas training course was held in Griffith in preparation for a possible chemical weapons attack on Dublin by one of the belligerents.

Just a year later, war did break out with Germany's invasion of Poland and Britain and France's subsequent declaration of war on Germany. However, it was the fall of France in 1940 that brought the reality of war close to neutral Ireland. Both Germany (looking for a way to attack Britain) and Britain (being anxious to regain control over the 'Treaty ports' of Cork, Berehaven and Lough Swilly which it had surrendered in 1938) drew up contingency plans for invading independent Ireland (popularly named Éire rather than the Free State since the 1937 constitution). To respond to these threats, the Irish Army had to be rapidly and quickly expanded for the duration of the war, or as it was called in Ireland, the Emergency.

A reserve, the Local Defence Force (LDF) was also established. The strength of the armed forces was temporarily brought up from about 13,000 in 1940 to some 41,000 for the duration of the war, with another 88,000 (mostly hastily trained and poorly equipped) men in the LDF. Several units of the LDF, including a contingent of 200 students from University College Dublin, were based in Griffith Barracks. The UCD contingent first paraded in Griffith in November 1941.

Effectively, therefore, there was a new 'Emergency Army'. A new battalion, the 14th, was raised and based in Griffith Barracks. The 14th was commanded by Colonel Joe Byrne with Commandant Kerins serving as second in Command. Many of the early recruits were veterans of the War of Independence and Civil War, who called themselves '[19]22 men'. To some extent, across the country, common service during the Emergency helped to heal the rifts caused by the Civil War, and so it was in Griffith. The 14th Battalion included Joe Dolan, the former IRA Squad man and National Army Intelligence Officer, who had once been described by one of his enemies as "the worst terrorist in Wellington barracks". Dolan had clearly not shed the ways of the gunman. He was described as "wearing his service revolver slung low on his thigh, he would stroll around the square in a detached manner", perhaps thinking of what he had done there during the Civil War.

His former enemy Joseph O'Connor, who had been held in Griffith Barracks during the Civil War, also served during the Emergency in the Local Defence Force (he was charged with guarding Government buildings in Merrion Street), as did many other former anti-Treatyites. Whether or not there was ever a personal reconciliation between Dolan and O'Connor, the fact that they were now wearing the same uniform did signify that the pain of the internecine conflict of 1922-23 was starting to recede.

Initially equipment was scarce and the soldiers in the 14th Battalion were issued with a mixture of equipment dating from the Great War, regular Army equipment and whatever else came to hand. The

Aftermath of the North Strand Bombings, 1941 – troops from Griffith were used in the rescue operation.
(Courtesy of the National Library of Ireland)

soldiers were charged with manning posts throughout Dublin each night. One hundred and fifty men, including detachments at banks, government buildings, the power station at Ringsend and elsewhere were on duty each night. Up to 1942, soldiers could sometimes have to do 100 hours duty each week. On occasion this guard duty included mounting a cordon in Seville Place in the north inner city for men wanted by the Gardaí. The most dangerous moments for Irish neutrality were in late 1940 and early 1941 when it appeared that a German invasion of Britain was imminent.

Throughout the autumn, winter and spring of 1940-1941, the Irish Army trained and prepared to repel an invasion from any quarter, whether an attack by British forces from Northern Ireland or a German airborne invasion in the south. When this did not transpire, the Irish Army was put to work at other tasks, including cutting turf, more of which was needed as a result of the war-enforced absence of coal. The soldiers based at Griffith were set to work cutting turf at Timahoe in County Laois and even won a turf cutting competition in Kildare in 1942. Another task in which they were employed was dealing with an outbreak of foot and mouth disease in 1941. Soldiers had to shoot the infected cattle and bury their corpses in trenches.

However, in the absence of foreign invasion, the most challenging work for the Emergency Army at Griffith proved to be rescue work in the aftermath of a German air raid in 1941.

In the early hours of January 3, 1941 it must have seemed for a moment that the war had come to Dublin. At 03.55 soldiers in Griffith were awakened by massive explosions as an aircraft dropped bombs on the South Circular Road, just yards from the perimeter of the barracks. Though the barracks was not hit, nearby houses were and the soldiers were among those who responded. For the next few hours they helped to rescue people trapped in the ruins of their houses. In all, 22 people were injured, none fatally. That night bombs were dropped on five counties in Ireland. In all cases, examination

Evening Herald, Friday January 3, 1941

of the bomb fragments proved that they had been dropped by German aircraft which were lost and had dumped their bomb-loads to lighten the aircraft. The Army's official statement read:

At 3:55 a.m. an unidentified aircraft dropped one bomb in Donore Terrace, South Circular Road, Dublin and destroyed two houses, seriously damaged a third and did slighter damage to the other houses in the area. Some twenty people were injured, but none seriously. The battalion of the Defence Forces stationed at Griffith Barracks turned out within a few minutes of the explosion and went to the aid of those who had been affected by the bombing'.

The Irish government made a formal complaint to Germany about the bombing, which like other German raids on Ireland are thought to have been mistakes on the part of German pilots. It was a small taste of war, one that anticipated the tragedy of the North Strand bombing a few months later on May 31, 1941. Troops from Griffith were mobilised to help victims in the North Strand, where 29 people were killed in the bombing, with 90 injured and 300 houses destroyed or damaged. Almost 400 people were left permanently or temporarily homeless.

Paying tribute to the service of the Emergency volunteers, the Minister for Defence Frank Aiken, addressing a parade of anti-air raid personnel at Griffith in 1944, told them that their voluntary service and unity had saved the country in the five disastrous years of war and had helped to preserve the national policy of neutrality. The 14th Battalion was demobilised at the war's end. Griffith Barracks was subsequently occupied by the 5th and 18th Infantry Battalions of the regular army from November to December 1946, but it then lay unoccupied by the military for several years.

In the meantime, the Labour Court occupied part of the barracks in 1947 as did the Office of Public Works or OPW from 1946 until 1966.

The barracks from the 1950s to the 1980s

In 1953, Griffith Barracks was reoccupied for military use by a new battalion under Commandant George Heffernan. With various parts of the complex in daily use by civilians, the normal military security precautions were compromised, as people going to and from the Labour Court wandered in and out. At one point Commandant Heffernan closed the gates and refused to let any civilians in until they could produce proof of their identity – an action that caused a minor sensation at the time. From this point onwards, a civilian messenger was posted on the gate to escort those making their way to the arbitration court.

In 1956 the IRA launched what they named 'Operation Harvest', better known as the 'Border Campaign', against targets in Northern Ireland. In response, the garrison at Griffith was ordered to send three reinforced companies to the border area to combat 'subversive activities' – in reality trying to impede the actions of the IRA. The IRA's campaign had run out of steam by 1961, but after 1969, when conflict again erupted within Northern Ireland, internal security within the Republic again became a priority.

In 1966, the Irish state commemorated the 50th anniversary of the Easter Rising of 1916. During Easter Week itself the Barracks, then known as Wellington, had been occupied by a small and rather scared garrison of British troops but had largely been left alone. In 1966 however, what was now Griffith Barracks was occupied by the Irish Army, which traced its ancestry back to those Volunteers who had sniped at Wellington in 1916. For the commemoration ceremony of the 1916 rising Colonel Ned Cusack led the 20th Battalion out of Griffith Barracks on Easter Sunday 1966 to the parade on O'Connell Street.

Of the 1966 parade, Cusack remembered:

The 20th Battalion FCA marched out the gate of the barracks down the South Circular Road to Harcourt Street and Dame Street passing the awaiting throngs in O'Connell Street, saluting the President on the GPO platform loaded with male and female VIPs and then marching back to Griffith via Camden Street and the South Circular Road. Tired and weary after a rather extended march, the 20th battalion on the march consisted of 4 companies (A, B, C, E) of about 120 men in each company – E Company (Complacht na bhFiann) conducted all its military training in Irish. All the battalion troops were Dublin City natives from all strata of society and I must say it was a great honour to lead such hard working, humorous and loyal young men. Incidentally, a commentary was broadcast by Miceal O'Hehir as the Army marched past the President at the GPO. Almost like a match broadcast in Croke Park!

In the 1970s, the Army was again expanded against the background of the Northern Ireland conflict and Griffith was again full, garrisoned by the 20th Battalion FCA and Motor Corps along with the 2nd Anti-Aircraft Battery, the 2nd Garrison Military Police Corps, Eastern Command Area Records, and the Observer Corps.

The FCA had previously been 'shadows' of Regular Battalions but from 1979 had autonomous units of their own. The Reserves, among them future President of Griffith College, Diarmuid Hegarty, then had a small cadre of Regulars who provided training and leadership during one training day per week at the barracks and one training day per month in the field.

1916 Jubilee Commemorations – parade and ceremonies at the General Post Office, Dublin. President Eamon de Valera, accompanied by Commandant Daniel O'Connell, inspects the Guard of Honour at the G.P.O. prior to the Military Parade. The Guard of Honour was furnished by the D Company 'The Pearse' 20th Infantry Battalion from Griffith Barracks.
(Courtesy of the Irish Photo Archive)

D Company 'The Pearse' members were practically all students, mainly from UCD, Clongowes, Newbridge, Belvedere, O'Connell Schools and De La Salle Churchtown. One of the Clongowes students was John Bruton, a subsequent Taoiseach.

The various civilian organisations based in Griffith, including the Labour Court, the Census of Population staff, the Dumping Body, and the Association of Parents and Friends of Mentally Handicapped Children, had to be relocated elsewhere, the last leaving in 1976.

The last Irish Army parade in Griffith Barracks on September 15th, 1988. The inspecting officers are Brigadier General Monahan, General Officer Commanding of the Eastern Command, escorted by Comandants McCann and Whelan and Captain Hynes, all of the Cavalry Squadron.

(Courtesy of An Cosantóir, 'Farewell to Griffith', September 1988)

The security risk posed to the state was highlighted by a shooting just outside Griffith Barracks on March 26, 1983. A sentry outside Griffith witnessed the shooting and fatal injuring of a prison officer, Brian Stack, who was shot by republican paramilitaries as he left the National Boxing Stadium, and died some months later.

Slums and Housing agitation

In 1962, Dublin Corporation took over some of the buildings at Griffith – the bank block and canteen, and used them for emergency housing for families from the inner city slums. At this time Dublin had a critical shortage of social housing and at its old core, a concentration of slum dwellings. Over 6,000 families were thought to live in overcrowded conditions and more lived in condemned buildings. The following year, the married quarters, which since 1924 had been leased by Greenmount and Boyne Linen Company for their workers, was also taken over by the corporation for use as emergency housing.

The accommodation at Griffith was to be used as a stop gap while decent housing was built elsewhere for families who had been living in condemned buildings in the city centre. Indeed, in one case in 1964, a family was housed in Griffith after the building they lived in collapsed altogether. By this time though, the old married quarters were in a very poor state of repair. What was more it had been decided that the housing at Griffith would only be used for women and children – their husbands and fathers would have to look elsewhere.

In 1963, there was a protest at Griffith about the poor conditions faced by the families housed there. In particular, the people living there objected to the fact that the husbands of families were not allowed to live in the accommodation. In December 1963, several men scaled the walls of Griffith to try to be with their families but were ordered out again by plainclothes policemen and officials of the Dublin Health Authority. In response, three families, the Quinns, the Flynns and the Morris's (a total of thirteen people) left the barracks and moved themselves into an abandoned house on nearby Clanbrassil Street. They alleged that they had been on the housing waiting list for five years.

In 1964, the Minster for Local Government, Neil Blaney, told the Dáil that 89 people were living in the Corporation-run housing at the Barracks, 23 women, 49 children and 17 men. In 1969, the Dublin Housing Action Committee were still complaining about the 'broken families' in Griffith and claimed that 14,000 new houses needed to be built in the Dublin Corporation area to clear effectively the inner city slums.

Nevertheless, it was not until the demands of the Irish Army required the return of the buildings in the barracks to military use that the last families moved out of Griffith in 1977.

By the late 1980s, the Irish Army decided to consolidate its barracks around the country and to shut some of its installations. The Army left Griffith in 1988, with the marching-out ceremony, on September 15th 1988, being presided over over by Commandant McCann of the Second Cavalry Squadron who presented his troops to Brigadier General P Monahan. The Cavalry Squadron moved to Cathal Brugha Barracks while the FCA units based in Griffith were moved to Cathal Brugha, Collins and McKee Barracks. The buildings then lay empty for a number of years.

Chapter 5
Arthur Griffith

Arthur Griffith departing for London from Dun Laoghaire for the Treaty Conference, 1921.
(Courtesy of the National Library of Ireland)

Arthur Griffith, after whom Wellington Barracks was renamed in 1923, was one of the most influential Irish nationalist leaders of his generation. Griffith was born in 1871 at 61 Upper Dominick Street, Dublin and was educated at the Christian Brothers' Schools at Strand Street and St Mary's Place. He worked as a printer, coming under the influence of the journalist and poet William Rooney, with whom he became active in the Gaelic League. He spent around two years in South Africa working in the gold mines there and editing a small English-language journal. He returned to Ireland in 1899 with the Boer War raging in South Africa and, perhaps radicalised by that conflict in which he had supported the Boers against the British Empire, he became more heavily involved in nationalist politics in Ireland. He became editor of the new weekly radical paper, the *United Irishman*, first published in Dublin in March 1899. In 1900, together with Rooney, he established an organisation named Cumann na nGaedheal.

In 1905 he established a separatist party known as Sinn Féin. Griffith argued, in a book entitled *The Resurrection of Hungary*, that Irish nationalists should model their search for independence on that of Hungary. There, elected representatives had seceded from the Austrian Habsburg parliament and set up their own parliament under the sovereignty of the Habsburg monarch. They had thus been recognised as equal parts of the Austro-Hungarian 'dual-monarchy'. In the same way, Griffith argued that Irish MPs should withdraw from Westminster and declare an Irish parliament in existence. A campaign of passive resistance might be necessary but ultimately Ireland could be an equal but separate part of a 'dual-monarchy'.

Sinn Féin's economic policy was based on making Ireland self-sufficient and the promotion of Irish industry. To this end, Griffith's newspaper *Sinn Féin* proposed such measures as Irish control over Irish banking and tariffs, the creation of an Irish merchant marine, reforestation, a return to tillage farming instead of 'ranching', and other policies designed to increase employment and make Ireland economically independent. Griffith was opposed to extreme radical labour and criticised the militant Transport Union leader James Larkin during the strike or 'lockout' of 1913, on the grounds that his methods would damage Irish trade.

However, Sinn Féin was initially quite unsuccessful. It had no Members of Parliament before 1917 and only a handful of county councillors, mostly in Dublin city, where its best result was getting 12 councillors elected in 1910 in an election where 80 seats were available. They briefly had one MP in 1908 when sitting MP in North Leitrim, Charles Dolan, resigned from the Irish Parliamentary Party and joined Sinn Féin, but he was subsequently defeated in a by-election.

The Irish Republican Brotherhood initially funded the *Sinn Féin* newspaper with money from Clan na

Gael in America, and for a time their activists campaigned for Sinn Féin in elections. From about 1910 though, coinciding with the growing influence of Tom Clarke and Seán McDermott who favoured armed insurrection, the organisation became increasingly disillusioned with electoral politics and instead concentrated on preparing for future armed revolt. Griffith was a member of the IRB, possibly up until 1910, after which time he generally eschewed the use of physical force for political ends.

Griffith opposed the involvement of Irishmen in the First World War on Britain's side and his newspaper was shut down and his printing press seized in late 1914. Griffith and Sinn Féin played no part in the Easter Rising of 1916 but he was nevertheless arrested after it and imprisoned in Reading Gaol together with other prominent separatists such as IRB man Ernest Blythe, Sinn Féin activist Herbert Moore Pim, labour organiser P.T. Daly, and the Cork Volunteer leaders Tomás MacCurtain and Terence MacSwiney. He was released, however, as part of the general amnesty of prisoners in December of 1916.

Once released, the veterans of the Rising, together with the pre-war Sinn Féin activists, coalesced in a new Sinn Féin party that would act as a vehicle for all radical nationalist politics. The new Sinn Féin had some continuity with Arthur Griffith's original party in that its principal strategy was to win elections in Ireland and having done that, to abstain from the Westminster Parliament, declare an Irish parliament to be in session and to secede from the United Kingdom. However, this Sinn Féin, after considerable internal debate, declared itself for an Irish Republic. Griffith declared himself agnostic on the subject of a republic and it was only in October 1917, and at the insistence of Collins, de Valera

Griffith and De Valera with other Treaty Plenipotentiaries on board the boat to England.
(Courtesy of the National Library of Ireland)

and other Rising veterans such as Cathal Brugha and Joseph McGuinness, that Sinn Féin pledged itself to the pursuit of an Irish Republic.

In 1917, the new Sinn Féin had its first electoral success when Count George Plunkett, father of Joseph, one of the executed leaders of 1916, won a by-election in Roscommon. Sinn Féin followed this victory up with two more in Counties Clare and Longford. This was the first in a string of by-election victories for Sinn Féin. In June 1918, Griffith himself was elected MP for East Cavan. In December 1918 the first general election after the First World War demonstrated that Irish opinion had swayed dramatically away from the Irish Parliamentary Party and towards Sinn Féin, who won 73 out of 105 seats. Griffith was returned unopposed for East Cavan. He was also elected, as was possible at the time, for Tyrone North West.

In January 1919, the Sinn Féin MPs met in Dublin's Mansion House and proclaimed that they had established an Irish Republic and that this assembly was the Dáil or Parliament of that republic. It was a stunning vindication for Griffith's political strategy. Griffith served as acting President of Dáil Éireann while Eamon de Valera toured America.

Griffith was known to be uneasy with the use of violence in the following years as the British authorities tried to suppress the republic and the Irish Republican Army or IRA attacked their police and military in Ireland. He was involved in several attempts to end the violence, conducting secret negotiations with the British throughout the War of Independence.

Arthur Griffith chatting to soldiers and civilians, c. 1922.
(Courtesy of the National Library of Ireland)

Firstly, in the summer of 1920, top British civil servants sent to Ireland, particularly a trio of Alfred Cope, Warren Fisher and John Anderson, recommended offering Dominion Status – the same autonomy enjoyed by Canada and Australia – to Sinn Féin. Through back channels, they communicated this to the Irish leadership and it appears that Arthur Griffith and Michael Collins viewed this compromise positively. However, the idea was not accepted at British cabinet level. It would not be until late 1921 and after a radical escalation of violence that such a proposal would be offered in earnest by the British side.

Secondly, in late 1920, secret talks, carried out via an intermediary between Lloyd George and Arthur Griffith, had produced the bones of another peace deal. Griffith presented the terms to Collins and the Dáil cabinet, who reacted favourably. A truce was scuppered, however, by Hamar Greenwood, the hard-line Chief Secretary for Ireland, who threatened to resign if there was a truce before the IRA surrendered its weapons. Griffith was imprisoned in December 1920 but was subsequently released on 30 June 1921. In July 1921, after six more months of violence, a truce was finally reached.

Griffith, Barton and Collins, December 1921.
(Courtesy of the National Library of Ireland)

Negotiations then began on a settlement to the question of Irish independence. Eamon de Valera declined to go to London for the negotiations and instead sent Arthur Griffith as head of the Irish negotiating team, along with Michael Collins, Eamon Duggan, Charles Gavan Duffy and Robert Barton. Erskine Childers went as secretary to the delegation.

The British refused to countenance an Irish Republic but instead offered an Irish Free State with dominion status. Northern Ireland (created in 1920) was given a period of a year to opt into or out of the Free State. The British also insisted that Irish members of parliament would have to take an oath of allegiance to the British monarch. Griffith advocated accepting the terms on the grounds that they gave the Irish state enough autonomy in fiscal, legal and military terms on which to build independence. However, when the negotiating team brought back the terms for the Dáil cabinet's perusal, the other members of the cabinet rejected it. De Valera told the negotiators that he might have been willing to compromise on either Irish unity or on unconditional independence, but 'you have got neither this nor that'. The meeting was brought to an end when Griffith proposed that they not sign the document in London but bring it back for the Dáil to vote on its acceptance.

Back in London on 4 December, Lloyd George told the Irish delegation it was either immediate signature or war and that he had to know by the next day. Collins and Griffith impressed on Barton, the last dissenter, that if he did not sign he alone would be responsible for a renewal of war. The Treaty was signed in the early morning of 6 December 1921.

While many of those who supported the Treaty did so on the basis that it was the best that could be achieved under the circumstances, Griffith defended it on its merits, arguing that 'we have brought back the flag, we have brought back the evacuation of Ireland after 700 years by British troops and the formation of an Irish Army. We have brought back to Ireland her full rights of fiscal control'.

On the Treaty's ratification by the Dáil, a Provisional Government, headed by Michael Collins and Arthur Griffith (who was named President of the Second Dáil), was set up to transfer power from the British administration to the Irish Free State.

When the Provisional Government and the Treaty settlement were threatened by a hardline anti-Treaty IRA grouping who had occupied the Four Courts in central Dublin in April 1922, Griffith argued from the start that they be removed by force. Collins, by contrast tried to conciliate the anti-Treatyites until late June 1922, when a combination of a desire to assert the authority of the Provisional Government, British pressure and anti-Treaty provocation forced his hand and he ordered the shelling of the Four Courts. In the subsequent Civil War between pro and anti-Treaty supporters, Griffith suffered severely from stress and had to be confined to a nursing home in August 1922. He resumed work as before but died of what was probably a heart attack (he was suffering from hypertension) on 12 August 1922. Just over a week later, his close colleague Michael Collins also died, killed in an ambush in County Cork.

Griffith was given a state funeral and later he and Collins (and then Kevin O'Higgins) were commemorated with a cenotaph in front of the new Irish parliament buildings at Leinster House. It later fell into poor repair and was pulled down, but was replaced by an obelisk in honour of the two men in 1956. Wellington Barracks was renamed Griffith Barracks in Arthur Griffith's honour in late 1922 or early 1923. Today Griffith is remembered as one of the founding fathers of the Irish state.

Chapter 6
From Barracks to College

Aerial view of Griffith College as it is today.

The departure of the stationed officers and their families in 1988, and the transfer of serving personnel to other Dublin barracks, effectively marked the end of the day-to-day activity at Griffith Barracks by the Irish Defence Forces. In the years that followed, most of the buildings were left completely unused, and with the passing of time, and no ongoing maintenance, they fell into considerable disrepair.

By 1990, the only remaining use being made of the barracks was of its medical centre to store archive material relating to the personal tax returns of Irish citizens. As the information was organised by county, the inclusion of the former names King's County, Queen's County and Co. Leix provided an insight into how regularly such information was being accessed.

Without further use for the barracks, the State decided to sell the central 6.7 acres of the site by public auction on 26th June 1991. Media commentators fully expected it to be acquired by developers for intensive housing and commercial retail use. Instead it was purchased for conversion to a third level college by Business and Accounting Training, at a cost of IR£1,750,000 (equivalent to €2,222,500). The acquisition of the Barracks was reported in the media as a 'new beginning', the auction by Fintan Gunne making RTÉ One's six o'clock news programme.

Directors of Griffith College, Pierce Kent, Professor Diarmuid Hegarty and Reg Callanan pictured after the purchase of the barracks.

The Conference Centre and Halls of Residence

Business and Accounting Training, or BAT as it was better known, was established by Diarmuid Hegarty in 1974 to prepare students for the professional examinations of the Institute of Chartered Accountants in Ireland. As a qualified accountant and barrister, working originally from his home, Diarmuid quickly established a reputation for excellent teaching and the examination successes achieved by his students.

During the late 1970s and early 1980s, Diarmuid, along with his co-directors Pierce Kent, Roderick Murphy, Frank Scott-Lennon and a small team of professional staff and lecturers, established the College's reputation as the premier provider of training leading to the professional examinations of the Institute of Chartered Accountants in Ireland (ACA). This achievement was clearly evidenced by the College's students taking first place in each of the final and penultimate examinations in 1983.

BAT was then joined by Reg Callanan, the College's Director of Professional Programmes, who extended the College's teaching into other professional accountancy bodies, both nationally with CPA and internationally with ACCA and CIMA. The College's rapid growth in numbers was supported by its move to rented premises initially in Milltown, subsequently in Ranelagh, and later in the acquisition of its own premises on Morehampton Road, Donnybrook.

By 1990, BAT's team and range of activities had extended beyond professional accountancy, with Edmond Holohan managing the delivery of certificate and diploma programmes in computing from City & Guilds and the National Computing Centre. Tomás Mac Eochagáin then joined the College as Director of Academic Programmes to introduce the College's degree programmes, starting with Computing Science in association with the University of Ulster (UU).

For Diarmuid and his colleagues in BAT, the State's auctioning of Griffith Barracks in June 1991 presented a unique opportunity. Where countless other buildings for sale in 1991 could have facilitated the College's expansion, Griffith Barracks was distinct in having the potential to provide third level students with a genuine campus experience. The site's character and ambience offered a vision of an ideal learning environment not dissimilar to the campuses of Trinity, NUI-Galway and UCC. There was plenty of space, listed buildings steeped in history, and it was located within and yet apart from Dublin's busy city centre.

Given the long established association of Arthur Griffith with Griffith Barracks, the College felt it appropriate that the link be continued into the future. Diarmuid Hegarty approached Ita Gray, only surviving child of Arthur Griffith, to ask her consent for a change of name to Griffith College in keeping with the naming of the barracks after her father. This request was granted by Ita and her family, thereby facilitating the transition of Business and Accounting Training to Griffith College Dublin, or GCD as it was to become better known.

From left: Lord Mayor Gay Mitchell, Shane Gray, Grandson of Arthur Griffith, Ita Gray, Daughter of Arthur Griffith and Diarmuid Hegarty President of Griffith College on the occasion of the announcement of the Griffith Scholarships on the 12th of August 1992.

View of the campus college green, c. 2000.

Being able to focus on the potential of the barracks was a necessary key motivation for GCD staff as they undertook to convert the site for use as a college. In particular, while the new location nominally offered a five-fold increase in teaching accommodation, many of the buildings were entirely unsuitable for occupation as the campus had become home in large part to foxes and pigeons. Reflecting on the move, long-term Griffith faculty member and head of Professional Accountancy, Ann Donegan, remembered how "the move from Morehampton Road to South Circular Road was both an exciting and scary leap for the staff at Griffith College as they faced the challenge of developing and modernising the campus".

The redevelopment of the College's existing buildings began in summer 1991. The first building to be refurbished was a three storey red brick addition built at the time of conversion from prison to barracks. This was refurbished at a cost of IR£180,000 and was then let to Tiernan Design School. To retain a link to the past, the building was renamed the Wellington building.

The old barracks medical centre continued to house revenue files for a period after the purchase. This lasted for about 18 months, during which continued the welcome presence of site security funded by the Exchequer. On vacation of the building by the Revenue Commissioners, it was converted to re-house the student restaurant and bar.

Refurbishment of the west block, renamed the Arthur Griffith Building, commenced in June 1992, with the firm Mahon McPhillips winning the tender and being awarded the contract. While plans were initially drawn up to develop both the west and the north blocks, work was restricted to the west block as the College, like the rest of the country, was hit by the credit crunch following the 1992 currency crisis.

By September 1992, the College began to transfer its own academic teaching activities from Morehampton Road to the South Circular Road. The commencement of activities in the newly refurbished sections of the College was marked by an opening ceremony, attended by Ita Gray and her family, at which a bust of Arthur Griffith was unveiled and mounted in the College's new reception area.

Business Expansion Scheme Proposal 1993.

To facilitate further re-development, the College raised IR£500,000 under the Business Expansion Scheme in April 1993 and a further IR£500,000 one year later. It also sold its properties on Morehampton Road, Donnybrook, the sale of which had been delayed by a collapse in property prices associated with the credit crunch. Under Reg Callanan's stewardship of the College as Managing Director during the 1990s, the College was enabled to fund further refurbishment of buildings from operational cash flow.

Work was also carried out on the grounds of the College with the planting of trees and the creation of a large central grass playing area, replacing the previously austere barracks square. These landscaping developments provided walkways for students, while also upgrading the College's electrical, plumbing and data communications networks to meet its growing needs. Having located their offices in the College, Conservation Volunteers Ireland developed an urban garden and tree nursery as a training site on campus. This work was officially launched in April 1993 by the President of Ireland, Mary Robinson.

While much development had yet to be undertaken, the sensitive refurbishment and revitalisation of historic buildings, along with the landscaping of the campus, showed how new life and function could be given to a vacated army barracks. The subsequent re-development of Collins' Barracks into the National Museum demonstrated another conservation success.

For Griffith College students, the move to the barracks represented a transformation of their College experience. The hugely increased space available provided freedom for students to meet and socialise,

President Mary Robinson officially launching the Conservation Volunteer Ireland Urban Project at Griffith College in April 1993.
(Image courtesy of the Irish Farmers Journal)

either through the various sports and social clubs or more generally by participating in the many social events held in the College's restaurant and bar. Academic resource developments included the provision of a professional library service under the care of Robert McKenna and his team, along with the ongoing development of computer laboratories. This transformation was captured in the College's marketing campaign at the time under the slogan 'College by Name – University by Nature'.

In tandem with the move to the Griffith College Campus and its continued development, the 1990s marked a period of considerable expansion for the College. It began with the development and growth of its degree and diploma programmes in Computing Science, Business Studies, and Accounting and Finance, all of which were validated by the University of Ulster. These programmes attracted a large cohort of students from Northern Ireland, creating an opportunity for students from all counties in Ireland to mix and study together towards common goals. For the period up to 1996, Northern Irish students also benefitted from the direct funding of their programmes by the UK government.

The success and reputation for quality of Griffith's degree programmes under the auspices of the University of Ulster demonstrated its unswerving commitment to quality, and in 1992, Seamus Brennan, TD and Minister for Education, officially approved Griffith College as a designated institution of the National Council for Educational Awards (NCEA). This led to the College offering a range of national certificate, national diploma and degree programmes under the auspices of the Irish Government. These programmes complemented the College's existing provision extending the range of programmes into interior design and law.

Former Griffith Barracks personnel meet with Prof. Diarmuid Hegarty on a visit to the campus in May 1995. Pictured (l-r): Prof. Diarmuid Hegarty, Cpl Thomas Kenny, Sgt John Griffin, Tpr Liam Dunne and Tpr Gerry Murdiff.
(Courtesy of An Cosantóir, Military Archives, Department of Defence)

Further government recognition of the College followed in 1999 with the Department of Enterprise and Employment funding the fees of students on the College's B.Sc. in Computing Science, and by doing so extending funding for the first time to an independent college. By the end of the decade, admission to the College's academic programmes was managed through the national CAO system alongside programmes from the State's universities and other third level institutions.

Throughout the mid-1990s, the College worked closely with Nottingham Trent University (NTU). This extended the range of degree programmes further to include Irish Law, Business and Law, and International Hospitality Management.

The developing campus on the South Circular Road, with its library, computer laboratories, student societies, restaurant and bar, attracted the interest of other related organisations resulting in many temporarily re-locating on campus. These included:

– The Law Society of Ireland, which renovated the top floor of the north block, now called the Daniel O'Connell building and ran their preparatory programmes in the College for a period of five years.
– Dublin's Anna Livia, radio station which established their radio broadcasting station on campus and remained on site for five years
– Brainwave – the Irish Epilepsy Association, which ran programmes for those with epilepsy integrating them into mainstream third level education

Even more significantly, several organisations came and stayed on campus, often through their integration with Griffith College. These organisations include:

- The Tiernan Design School which became the College's Design Faculty
- Newman College's Journalism School which relocated its programmes in journalism to Griffith College and began the College's Journalism and Media Faculty.
- Allied Computer Training and Advanced Technology Training, whose students progressed to Griffith College following the closure of their organisations in the mid-1990s.
- Dublin International Foundation College, which offers its own suite of foundation and university preparation programmes to international third level students.

In 1998, the College integrated the Leinster School of Music and Drama (LSMD) as a constituent school within Griffith College. Established in 1904, the LSMD already had a longstanding tradition of excellent teaching, along with the preparation of teachers nationwide. It also conducted graded examinations nationwide, with over 15,000 students taking their examinations annually. Joining the College brought students of drama, classical and traditional music and opera together with the rest of an increasingly diverse student body.

Being part of Griffith College, the development of the LSMD led to the provision of Higher Diploma programmes in both Music Education and Drama Education along with the recognition of its grades by Quality and Qualifications, Ireland (QQI). At the same time, it preserved the School's historic links with its past through the continued use of its Teacher Diploma Parchments designed by Grace Plunkett, the Irish artist and cartoonist who was active in the Republican movement, and who married Joseph Plunkett in Kilmainham Goal only a few hours before he was executed for his part in the 1916 Easter Rising.

By the end of the 1990s, under the marketing direction of Ronan Fenelon, the College had experienced considerable growth in the number of Irish students attending its courses. From 1994 onwards, recruitment of international students was to become a key component of the growth of the College. Students were recruited from as near as Northern Ireland and Norway to as far as China, India and Pakistan. Indeed, Griffith College was the first higher education institution to recruit directly in China under the enterprising direction of Leo O'Brien, the College's International Marketing Director.

21st Century at Griffith College

While the 1990s had focused on the redevelopment of existing barrack buildings, the first years of the new millennium brought even greater changes to the campus with the development of new facilities for staff and students.

In June 2000, a modern glass structure known as the link block was completed at a cost of IR£215,000. This provided direct internal connection between the west and north blocks, now named after Arthur Griffith and Daniel O'Connell respectively.

The Griffith College Halls of Residence which were built to complement the original buildings.

The College then embarked on its most ambitious development to date - planning, commissioning and financing the development of purpose built on-campus student accommodation for its students.

In October 2002, the College obtained planning permission on appeal from An Bord Pleanála to construct two student accommodation blocks providing accommodation for 664 students, permission having been originally refused by Dublin City Council. In support of the appeal, An Bord Pleanála received a record number of 38 submissions favouring the development. Demolition of a number of old buildings started in August 2003 with both blocks completed by March 2005 at a cost of €36 million.

Designed by Aidan Powell, architect and built by P.J Hegarty & Sons, the accommodation blocks are architecturally sympathetic to the original buildings on campus with the added advantage of providing extensive underground car parking facilities. As the students staying in the Halls of Residence rarely required parking spaces, the largely unused facility proved a most welcome bonus for the College's other full-time and part-time students.

During the construction phase, some of the College's teaching and administrative activities were relocated to modular buildings newly acquired from the National College of Ireland as it relocated from Ranelagh to the city centre. Catering and examination facilities were also provided by the neighbouring National Stadium.

By the mid-2000s, it was clear that the College needed additional teaching, examining and catering facilities to meet the needs of its growing Irish and international student body. This led to the development of the College's Conference Centre, by the same design and construction teams that worked on the Halls of Residence. Construction began in March 2005 and was completed in March 2006 at the cost of €15.8 million. As part of the new complex, the College also built a dedicated design facility. The new buildings were officially opened by An Taoiseach Bertie Ahern on 25th September 2006.

This large scale development of modern buildings marked a significant expansion in the College's footprint on site. Included in the construction of the Conference Centre building was a 650 seat auditorium that could be converted readily to accommodate exhibitions, examinations and graduations. Equally, it allowed for its rearrangement as three large lecture theatres.

Other floors of the building provide conference facilities, additional lecture theatres and administrative offices. The entire basement floor is used for the College's restaurant and bar. Following a poll by students and staff, the new bar and restaurant facility was named Arthur's, presumably in memory of Arthur Griffith.

By the late 2000s, the Griffith College student experience had been transformed. The College now had over 600 students living on campus and a flourishing Students' Union which ensured strong student engagement in the College's societies and sporting clubs. For full-time students, the student experience went beyond the end of the last lecture at 5pm, as they could now continue to enjoy the College environs, for social, sporting and, of course, study purposes long into the evening. Furthermore, the College's student population had become increasingly enriched and diverse with the presence of students from up to 60 countries.

Even during the summer months, when many colleges fall quiet, the College and its Halls of Residence are alive with hundreds of overseas students attending English language summer camp courses with the College's English language school. In undertaking such projects the College has been fortunate to have always had a strong team of qualified accountants on its board to manage the finances involved under the careful direction of Pat Sheehan, the College's finance director.

In remarking on the journey undertaken by the College following the completion of the buildings, Pierce Kent summed up the moves as follows: "From little acorns...! From a basement in Miltown Park, to a Georgian terrace in Ranelagh, to a former An Óige hostel in Donnybrook, to a bona fide campus in Griffith Barracks. At last... a facility fitting as a seat of education and learning!"

The development of the College's buildings could never have been realised without the parallel successful development of the College's academic and professional programmes managed by the College's heads of faculty, programme directors, lecturers and staff.

As Managing Director since 2000, Tomás Mac Eochagáin guided the further development of the College's educational provision and quality assurance systems. In the case of the College's academic programmes, this development led to a major strengthening of the academic qualifications and related research activities of faculty staff resulting in the provision of postgraduate and master's level programmes in computing, business, law, media, design and education. This period in the College's history also saw a considerable diversification of the core disciplines being delivered to include photography, fashion, hospitality management, film, sound engineering, digital technology, computer games and music production.

These developments led to closer links with industry and employers, and enhanced the preparedness of learners for the workplace, with students regularly winning national and international professional awards. Further direct links with other organisations were established through the joint development of accredited programmes with the Irish Small and Medium Enterprise Association (ISME), the Institute of Certified Public Accountants of Ireland (CPA), Windmill Lane Academy, and Globe Business College in Munich. The College also established Clarus Press, a legal publishing company for specialist publications and peer reviewed law journals.

External research projects undertaken during this period included the annual International Conference for Engaging Pedagogy (ICEP) established under the guiding hand of Fiona O'Riordan, head of the College's Centre for Promoting Academic Excellence, and the Innocence Project which seeks to exonerate victims of miscarriages of justice, established by David Langwallner, Dean of the College's Law School.

The period from 2005 on saw the College extend its provision to Cork and Limerick through the acquisition of Skerry's Business College in Cork in 2005 and the Mid-West Business Institute, Limerick in 2006. Both colleges had previously established an excellent reputation for providing third level programmes under the auspices of the Higher Education and Training Awards Council (HETAC). Working together, sharing the best of their combined experience, allowed all centres to provide a wider and improved service to students. From 2006 onwards, the College adopted the name Griffith College in place of the former Griffith College Dublin.

The 2000s was also a most successful period for the College's professional programmes with its centres in Dublin, Cork and Limerick achieving Gold and later Platinum Status with the Association of Chartered Certified Accountants (ACCA) in respect of their teaching quality. This recognition was directly reflected in the ongoing national and worldwide prizewinning places achieved by the College's students.

Starting in 2004, the Griffith College Distinguished Fellowship and Professional Excellence Awards were the brainchild of Prof Wallace Ewart former Pro Vice Chancellor of the University of Ulster and long-time mentor of Griffith College. The Distinguished Fellowship Award was established to recognise a major contribution at national or international level in the fields of business and public administration.

The College's Distinguished Fellowship Award holders to date include:

Seamus Heaney, MRIA, Poet and Nobel Laureate

John Hume, KCSG, Nobel Peace Laureate, SDLP Leader, MP and MEP

Mary McAleese, President of Ireland

The Hon. Mrs. Justice Susan Denham, Chief Justice of Ireland

Catherine Day, Secretary General of the EU Commission

Professor Richard Barnett, Vice Chancellor, University of Ulster

Diljit Rana, Baron Rana, MBE, Member of the House of Lords

Peter Sutherland KCMG, SC, Attorney General and EU Commissioner

Denis O'Brien, MBA, Chairman, Communicorp Group Ltd

Martin Naughton, Founder and Chairman, Glen Dimplex Group

Gillian Bowler, Founder Budget Travel and Chairman, Fáilte Ireland

Edward Haughey, Baron Ballyedmond, OBE, Member of Seanad Eireann and the House of Lords, Founder and Chairman, Norbrook Laboratories Ltd.

The Professional Excellence Award was established to recognise excellent performance in their chosen profession of recipients of the award. Since its establishment there have been 14 recipients:

Mr Michael Cawley, Deputy Chief Executive, Chief Operating Officer, Ryanair

Dr Martin Newell, Former CEO, Central Applications Office

Mr Terence O'Rourke, Managing Partner, KPMG

Ms Sylvia Meehan, First Chairperson and Chief Executive of the Employment Equality Agency and Former President of the Irish Senior Citizens Parliament

Mr Paul Rellis, Managing Director, Microsoft

Fr Peter McVerry SJ, Founder, Peter McVerry Trust for Dublin Homeless

Mr Louis Copeland, Master Tailor

Mr George Hook, Journalist and Broadcaster

Mr Kevin Moran, Gaelic and Soccer Footballer

Mr John Bowman, Journalist, Broadcaster and Historian

Griffith College Distinguished Fellowship Award Recipients

Professor Richard Barnett
Vice Chancellor, University of Ulster
Distinguished Fellow 2014

The Hon. Mrs Justice Susan Denham
Chief Justice of Ireland
Distinguished Fellow 2013

Seamus Heaney MRIA
Poet & Nobel Laureate
Distinguished Fellow 2012

Peter Sutherland KCMG, SC
Attorney General & EU Commissioner
Distinguished Fellow 2011

Catherine Day
Sec. General of the EU Commission
Distinguished Fellow 2010

Diljit Rana, Baron Rana, MBE
Member of House of Lords
Distinguished Fellow 2009

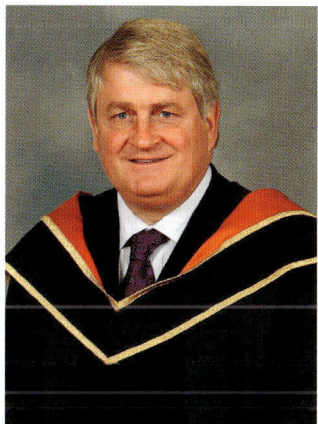
Denis O'Brien, MBA
Chairman, Communicorp Group Ltd
Distinguished Fellow 2008

Mary McAleese
President of Ireland
Distinguished Fellow 2007

John Hume, KCSG
Nobel Peace Laureate
Distinguished Fellow 2006

Martin Naughton
Founder & Chairman,
Glen Dimplex Group
Distinguished Fellow 2006

Gillian Bowler
Founder, Budget Travel &
Chairman, Failte Ireland
Distinguished Fellow 2005

Edward Haughey,
Baron Ballyedmond, OBE
Member Seanad Eireann and House of Lords
Founder & Chairman, Norbrook Laboratories
Distinguished Fellow 2004

Mr Frank Ryan, Founder Member of Society for Designers (now the Institute of Designers in Ireland)

Dr Veronica Dunne, Internationally acclaimed opera singer, Royal Irish Academy of Music and Leinster School of Music and Drama

Mr Richard Roche, Journalist, Author, Member of Irish Council for the Training of Journalists and Founder of Griffith College Journalism School

Ms Sheila Murphy, Director, Leinster School of Music and Drama

In 2004, the College's higher education programmes were placed on Ireland's National Framework of Qualifications (NFQ), and subsequently the College had its quality assurance procedures agreed with HETAC. This led to the constitution of the College's Academic and Professional Council (APC) which became the custodian of the College's standards governing its streams of academic and professional training activities. In 2008, while maintaining its board of managers, the College adopted the nomenclature more in common with other academic institutions of president and directors of function.

In 2009, HETAC undertook a comprehensive external review of the entire College encompassing its academic and administrative procedures. This quality audit commended the College on its Quality Assurance Procedures and their effectiveness. It also confirmed that for students, the College's greatest strength lay in the quality and approachability of its lecturing and administrative team.

Following the review, and in recognition of HETAC's confidence in the quality of the College's staff and procedures, HETAC devolved to the College many of the processes it previously reserved for itself in relation to the validation and re-validation of its programmes of study.

Recognising the College's significant presence in the Chinese market, Prof Diarmuid Hegarty in 2012 was awarded an honorary professorship from the Beijing Information, Science and Technology University in China.

In line with the College's increasing experience of both international students and quality assurance systems, it led the development of quality standards for the provision of international education on behalf of the IHEQN, the Irish Higher Education Quality Network. Established in 2003, the IHEQN provides a forum for the discussion of quality assurance and quality improvement issues amongst the principal national stakeholders involved in the quality assurance of higher education and training in Ireland. Currently chaired by Professor Diarmuid Hegarty of Griffith College, the network's members include the Irish Universities Association, Institutes of Technology Ireland, the Department of Education and Science, the Royal College of Surgeons, Quality and Qualifications Ireland and the Higher Education Authority.

The Academic Year 2013/14

The commencement of the 2013/14 academic year marks the 40th anniversary of Griffith College. Since its foundation, the College has grown to become Ireland's largest private third-level college with over 7,000 students at its campuses in Dublin, Cork and Limerick. The year also marks Griffith College's move to larger campuses in Cork and Limerick.

In delivering the programmes, a total of over 400 specialist and professional staff commit themselves to the educational and personal development of the College's learners, to their own development and that of the College. Of those, almost 200 do so on a full-time basis. Without this team and the support of external agencies such as the QQI, HEA, NTU, UU and the professional examination bodies, Griffith College would simply not survive, let alone prosper.

Griffith College Limerick.

FROM BARRACKS TO COLLEGE

Griffith College Cork.

The current profile of the students stands in certain contrast to that of the first classes offered by Diarmuid Hegarty back in 1974. While continuing to teach professional accountancy along with a wide range of professional and academic programmes, the College's courses have expanded further into new areas to include government funded programmes in digital marketing and cloud computing. Thanks to the College's partnerships with over 140 universities and higher education institutions internationally, it now welcomes students from over 77 countries, further enriching student life for all. France, Germany, China, India, Norway, the US and Brazil are just some of the main countries from which the College's students are drawn. This mix of Irish and international students on campus has added considerably to the learning experience of all cohorts, providing an experience and understanding of different cultures invaluable in today's global economy.

As in previous years, the College continues to nurture successful prizewinning students. While some will secure such recognition during their years at the College, others will inevitably become famous in their subsequent careers, perhaps following in the footsteps of recent alumni like the writer Cecila Ahern, TD Helen McEntee, presenter Laura Whitmore, and journalists Chris Donoghue and Henry McKean, along with several former past presidents of professional accountancy bodies and CEOs of multinational companies.

Looking back further into the alumni of Griffith's constituent colleges, they may even become another Taoiseach (Jack Lynch – Skerry's Business College), or Nobel Laureate (Samuel Beckett – Leinster School of Music and Drama).

To students entering Griffith College in 2013/14, the campus presents a lively sight of optimistic and talented students from many countries pursuing higher education. Perhaps only a few will ever be aware of those who shared the same ground before them, as students, soldiers or prisoners during the 200 years of history which are encapsulated within the historic campus.

It will be difficult for new students to recall that hundreds of prisoners were once kept here for minor crimes, that two men were executed and buried here in unmarked graves in the 19th century, and that the barracks witnessed violence and bloodshed throughout the Easter Rising, Anglo-Irish War and more especially in the Civil War, when hundreds of prisoners were again incarcerated in its buildings. In naming the College's buildings after Griffith, O'Connell, Meagher, Stephens, Wellington and others, the College wishes to respect and preserve the campus' links with its history.

For the most part, it can be expected that students will be busy building their own memories and creating a continuing history for the College based around their many friendships, the events they have enjoyed, and the time they spent advancing their careers in the company of others. In doing so, it is hoped that when they have opportunities to reflect on their own journeys, they will look back fondly on their experience at Griffith College and regard it as one of the most enjoyable and successful parts of their lives.

Bibliography

Primary Sources

Reports from Commissioners, Session, Vol. XXXVI, Prisons, Scotland and Ireland, January 24 – August 28, 1860

Return to the House of Commons on Richmond Bridewell Dublin Expenditure, 18 August 1892. (Digitised University of Southampton)

Report on Richmond Bridewell, Appendix to 49th Report of Commissioners on Prisons (Ireland and Scotland), Vol. XXX, 9 February – 21 August 1871

National Archive 1911 census

Military Census 1922

Parliamentary Debates

Criminal Law and Procedure (Ireland) Act – Arrest of Members – House of Commons Debate February 9, 1888

Dáil Éireann – Ceisteanna – 13 September, 1922, Military Prisoners.

Dáil Éireann – Volume 1 – 04 October, 1922, Treatment of Prisoners.

Bureau of Military History

Eamon Broy, WS 1,284

Cahir Davitt WS 1751

Gerard Doyle WS 1511

Kit Farrell WS 1299

Edward Handley WS 625

Robert Holland WS 280

Seamus Kavanagh WS 493

Thomas McCarthy WS 307

Joseph McGuiness WS 607

Joseph O'Connor WS 157, 487, 544

Padraig O'Connor WS 813

Journal articles

Comdt. P.D. O'Donnell, *Griffith Barracks Dublin, Barracks and Post of Ireland*, No 28, An Cosantoir, November 1978.

P.D. O'Donnell, *Griffith Barracks Dublin, Barracks and Post of Ireland* No 29 , An Cosantoir, January 1979

Doyle, Rob, National Graves Association entry on Joseph Poole, online at http://www.nga.ie/Fenians-Joseph_Poole.php http://paperspast.natlib.govt.nz/cgi-bin/paperspast?a=d&d=CHP18840114.2.21.4

Durney, James, *How Aungier/ Camden Street became known as the Dardanelles*, The Irish Sword, Summer 2010 No. 108 Vol. XXVII

Kinsella, Anthony, *The British Evacuation*, The Irish Sword, No. 82

Walsh, Paul V, *The Irish Civil War, a study of the Conventional phase*, A paper delivered to NYMAS at the CUNY Graduate Center, New York, N.Y. on 11 December 1998

Books

Balthrop, Micheal, *The Old Contemptibles*, Osprey 1989.

Carroll-Burke, Patrick, *Colonial Discipline, The Making of the Irish Convict System*, Four Courts Press, Dublin 2000.

Geoghegan, Patrick, *Liberator, The Life and Death of Daniel O'Connell,1830-1847*, Gill & MacMillan, Dublin 2010.

Hopkinson, Michael, *Green Against Green, The Irish Civil War*, Gill & MacMillan, Dublin 2004.

Kennerk, Barry, *Shadow of the Brotherhood, The Temple Bar Shootings*, Mercier Press, Cork 2010.

Laird, Frank, *Personal Experiences of the Great War*, Eason and Sons, 1925.

Lewis, Samuel, *A Topographical Dictionary of Ireland*, London, 1837.

MacDonald, Lyn, *1914, The Days of Hope*, Penguin 1987.

McManus, Ruth, *Shaping Dublin City and Suburbs, 1910-1940*, Four Courts Press, Dublin 2002.

O'Connor, Diarmuid and Connolly, Frank, *Sleep Soldier Sleep, The Life and Times of Padraig O'Connor*, Miseab, Dublin 2011.

O Grada, Cormac, *Black '47 and Beyond, The Great Irish Famine in History and Memory*, Princeton University Press, New Jersey, 1999.

Sheehan, William, *Fighting for Dublin, The British Battle for Dublin*, Collins Press, Cork 2008.

Vaughan, W.E, *Murder Trials in Ireland 1836-1914*, Four Courts Press, Dublin, 2009.

Yeates, Padraig, *Dublin, A City in Wartime 1914-1918*, Gill & MacMillan, Dublin 2011.

The Wolfe Tone Annual 1962.

Newspapers

The Irish Times archive

New York Times archive

Imagery and photography sources

National Library of Ireland, Kildare Street, Dublin 2

Ordnance Survey Ireland, Phoenix Park, Dublin 8

Irish Photo Archive Ltd. 17 Nottingham St, North Strand, Dublin 3

Irish Farmers Journal, Irish Farm Centre, Bluebell, Old Nace Road, Dublin 12

Christian Brothers, Edmund Rice House, North Richmond St., Dublin 1

Military Archives, Cathal Brugha Barracks, Military Rd, Dublin 6

Harpers Weekly

Robert Delaney

Irish Architectural Archive, 45 Merrion Square, Dublin 2